Pilgrim People

Pilgrim People

Clifford M. Yeary
with Little Rock Scripture Study staff

Little Rock
Scripture Study

LITURGICAL PRESS
Collegeville, Minnesota

www.littlerockscripture.org

Nihil obstat: Reverend Robert Harren, J.C.L., *Censor deputatus.*
Imprimatur: ✠ Most Reverend Donald J. Kettler, J.C.L., Bishop of Saint Cloud, October 29, 2019.

Cover design by John Vineyard. Interior art by Ned Bustard. Photo on page 25 courtesy of iStockphoto.com. Maps on pages 14, 42, and 51 created by Robert Cronan of Lucidity Information Design, LLC.

 This symbol indicates material that was created by Little Rock Scripture Study to supplement the biblical text and commentary. Some of these inserts first appeared in the *Little Rock Catholic Study Bible*; others were created specifically for this book by Michael DiMassa.

1   2   3   4   5   6   7   8   9

Library of Congress Cataloging-in-Publication Data

Names: Yeary, Clifford M., author. | Little Rock Scripture Study Staff, author.
Title: Pilgrim people / Clifford M. Yeary with Little Rock Scripture Study Staff.
Description: Collegeville, MN : Liturgical Press, 2020. | Series: Little Rock scripture study | Includes
   bibliographical references. | Summary: "A Bible study focusing on four major pilgrimages in Scripture-
   the journey of trust with Abraham and Sarah, the journey of freedom with Moses and the Hebrew
   people, the journey of exile and return with Israel, and the journey of discipleship with Jesus and his
   followers"—Provided by publisher.
Identifiers: LCCN 2019043216 (print) | LCCN 2019043217 (ebook) | ISBN 9780814665282 (paperback) |
   ISBN 9780814665046 (epub) | ISBN 9780814665046 (mobi) | ISBN 9780814665046 (pdf)
Subjects: LCSH: Yeary, Clifford M. Pilgrim people. | Christian pilgrims and pilgrimages—Textbooks. |
   Spiritual formation—Textbooks. | Pilgrims and pilgrimages in the Bible.
Classification: LCC BV5067 .Y433 2020 (print) | LCC BV5067 (ebook) | DDC 262/.7—dc23
LC record available at https://lccn.loc.gov/2019043216
LC ebook record available at https://lccn.loc.gov/2019043217

TABLE OF CONTENTS

Wrap-Up Lectures and Discussion Tips for Facilitators are available for each lesson at no charge. Find them online at LittleRockScripture.org/Lectures/PilgrimPeople.

Welcome

The Bible is at the heart of what it means to be a Christian. It is the Spirit-inspired word of God for us. It reveals to us the God who created, redeemed, and guides us still. It speaks to us personally and as a church. It forms the basis of our public liturgical life and our private prayer lives. It urges us to live worthily and justly, to love tenderly and wholeheartedly, and to be a part of building God's kingdom here on earth.

Though it was written a long time ago, in the context of a very different culture, the Bible is no relic of the past. Catholic biblical scholarship is among the best in the world, and in our time and place, we have unprecedented access to it. By making use of solid scholarship, we can discover much about the ancient culture and religious practices that shaped those who wrote the various books of the Bible. With these insights, and by praying with the words of Scripture, we allow the words and images to shape us as disciples. By sharing our journey of faithful listening to God's word with others, we have the opportunity to be stretched in our understanding and to form communities of love and learning. Ultimately, studying and praying with God's word deepens our relationship with Christ.

Pilgrim People

The resource you hold in your hands is divided into four lessons. Each lesson involves personal prayer and study using this book *and* the experience of group prayer, discussion, and wrap-up lecture.

If you are using this resource in the context of a small group, we suggest that you meet four times, discussing one lesson per meeting. Allow about 90 minutes for the small group gathering. Small groups function best with eight to twelve people to ensure good group dynamics and to allow all to participate as they wish.

Some groups choose to have an initial gathering before their regular sessions begin. This allows an opportunity to meet one another, pass out books, and, if desired, view the optional intro lecture for this study available on the "Resources" page of the Little Rock Scripture Study website (www.littlerockscripture.org).

Every Bible study group is a little bit different. Some of our groups like to break each lesson up into two weeks of study so they are reading less each week and have more time to discuss the questions together at their weekly gatherings.

If your group wishes to do this, simply agree how much of each lesson will be read each week, and only answer the questions that correspond to the material you read. Wrap-up lectures can then be viewed at the end of every other meeting rather than at the end of every meeting. Of course, this will mean that your study will last longer, and your group will meet more times.

WHAT MATERIALS WILL YOU USE?

The materials in this book include:

- Commentary by Clifford M. Yeary, which has also been published separately as *Pilgrim People: A Scriptural Commentary* (Liturgical Press).
- Occasional inserts 🔥 highlighting elements of the New and Old Testaments. Some of these appear also in the *Little Rock Catholic Study Bible* while others are supplied by staff writers.
- Questions for study, reflection, and discussion at the end of each lesson.
- Opening and closing prayers for each lesson, as well as other prayer forms available in the closing pages of the book.

In addition, there are wrap-up lectures available for each lesson. Your group may choose to purchase a DVD containing these lectures or make use of the audio or video lectures online at no charge. The link to these free lectures is: LittleRockScripture.org/Lectures/PilgrimPeople. Of course, if your group has access to qualified speakers, you may choose to have live presentations.

Each person will need a current translation of the Bible. We recommend the *Little Rock Catholic Study Bible*, which makes use of the New American Bible, Revised Edition. Other translations, such as the New Jerusalem Bible or the New Revised Standard Version: Catholic Edition, would also work well.

HOW WILL YOU USE THESE MATERIALS?

Prepare in advance

Using Lesson One as an example:

- Begin with a simple prayer like the one found on page 11.

- Read the assigned material in the printed book for Lesson One (pages 12–25) so that you are prepared for the weekly small group session. You may do this assignment by reading a portion over a period of several days (effective and manageable) or by preparing all at once (more challenging).

- Answer the questions, Exploring Lesson One, found at the end of the assigned reading, pages 26–28.

- Use the Closing Prayer on page 29 when you complete your study. This prayer may be used again when you meet with the group.

Meet with your small group

- After introductions and greetings, allow time for prayer (about 5 minutes) as you begin the group session. You may use the prayer found on page 11 (also used by individuals in their preparation) or use a prayer of your choosing.

- Spend about 45–50 minutes discussing the responses to the questions that were prepared in advance. You may also develop your discussion further by responding to questions and interests that arise during the discussion and faith-sharing itself.

- Close the discussion and faith-sharing with prayer, about 5–10 minutes. You may use the Closing Prayer at the end of each lesson or one of your choosing at the end of the book. It is important to allow people to pray for personal and community needs and to give thanks for how God is moving in your lives.

- Listen to or view the wrap-up lecture associated with each lesson (15–20 minutes). You may watch the lecture online, use a DVD, or provide a live lecture by a qualified local speaker. This lecture provides a common focus for the group and reinforces insights from each lesson. You may view the lecture together at the end of the session or, if your group runs out of time, you may invite group members to watch the lecture on their own time after the discussion.

Above all, be aware that the Holy Spirit is moving within and among you.

Pilgrim People

LESSON ONE

The Call of Abraham and Sarah

Begin your personal study and group discussion with a simple and sincere prayer such as:

Prayer

God, you are the source and goal of all life. Strengthen, support, and guide us on our earthly pilgrimage so that, nourished by your word and inspired by your Son's example, we may persevere in faith until we find ourselves home at last in your heavenly kingdom.

Read the Introduction and pages 12–25, Lesson One.

Respond to the questions on pages 26–28, Exploring Lesson One.

The Closing Prayer on page 29 is for your personal use and may be used at the end of group discussion.

INTRODUCTION

What does it mean today to be part of a people whose very identity is rooted in the belief that they belong to God and that their lives are a pilgrimage of faith?

It is a statement of faith among the Jewish people, embedded in the covenant God made with them through Moses: "My father was a wandering Aramean" (Deut 26:5).

This wandering father of the Jews is most probably Jacob, the grandson of Abraham and Sarah. Considering Abraham and Sarah's own journey of faith, Jacob was by no means the first person in the story of their covenant to be a wanderer. Jacob, however, has the distinction of being renamed "Israel" after wrestling with a divine messenger on the banks of the river Jabbok; as Israel he becomes the model of a people who both wander and wrestle with God.

As understood for millennia within the Judeo-Christian heritage, Abraham, with Sarah, his wife, set forth on a journey of faith that would come to exemplify the very nature of faith. They abandoned a home in response to a spiritual call and journeyed toward a land God promised to give their descendants. Their faith in the promise was not entirely for their own benefit. First, this childless couple had to trust in God as they grew older and older that they would even have offspring. Then, they had to trust that the promise of the land would be fulfilled by this same God long after they died.

Paul assured the Christians of ancient Rome that they were the spiritual offspring of Abraham (Rom 4:1-17), and so Christians have always regarded themselves as children of Abraham. Like Abraham, we are also sojourners in a land that is not truly our home, for "our citizenship is in heaven" (Phil 3:20), and like Abraham, we are "looking forward to the city with foundations, whose architect and maker is God" (Heb 11:10). We can look forward to it in faith and hope because so much of its joy has already filled our hearts (see Rom 5:1-5).

Through the broad, colorful strokes of the Bible, from Genesis through the New Testament, this commentary will explore important dimensions of what it means to be a people who belong to God and whose lives are a pilgrimage of faith. For every believer, however, it also means something intensely personal. It is a personal journey of faith that each one of us is set upon, but Scripture can shed a much needed spiritual light on our personal journeys.

THE CALL OF ABRAHAM AND SARAH

Who Was Called First?

Genesis 11:31–12:3

^{11:31}Terah took his son Abram, his grandson Lot, son of Haran, and his daughter-in-law Sarai, the wife of his son Abram, and brought them out of Ur of the Chaldeans, to go to the land of Canaan. But when they reached Haran, they settled there. ³²The lifetime of Terah was two hundred and five years; then Terah died in Haran.

^{12:1}The LORD said to Abram: "Go forth from the land of your kinsfolk and from your father's house to a land that I will show you.

²"I will make of you a great nation,
 and I will bless you;
I will make your name great,
 so that you will be a blessing.
³I will bless those who bless you
 and curse those who curse you.
All the communities of the earth
 shall find blessing in you."

The most significant thing about Terah is not that he lived to be two hundred and five. Life spans in Genesis are frequently reported in numbers that are frankly inexplicable, but our incredulity should not get in the way of hearing the inspired message. There is a Samaritan version of this text that says Terah only lived to be one hundred and forty-five (only!). Regardless, we are meant to understand that although Terah lived a good long while, he had at one time set out from Ur for Canaan with Abram and Sarai and Lot. This is before Genesis tells us that Abram and Sarai received their own call to resume the journey to Canaan.

Ur appears to have been in what is now modern Iraq, along the Euphrates, perhaps near the ancient shore of the Persian Gulf. Today this is where the Euphrates and the Tigris rivers flow together into a delta that has pushed out the shore for many miles.

Had God called Terah to make this journey first? The text leaves that for us to ponder without an answer. But consider this: Terah had set out for Canaan with the same people in tow that God would later call to complete that journey. Whether or not Terah heard a call from God, it was God's intention that the journey should be completed. When Terah stopped short and settled in Haran they had completed a good part of the journey. Haran was probably located in the southeast of what is now modern Turkey, north of Syria. A turn to the south would have eventually taken Terah to Canaan.

If God did call Terah to leave Ur and to travel to Canaan, close would not have been good enough—not if he still had strength to venture toward the goal. The text is clear on this: Terah *settled* in Haran. He had made Haran his home. His journey to Canaan had not just been delayed, he had found a place to call home. Now the journey he had begun would have to be taken up by others.

That is when God calls Abram and Sarai to resume the journey that began in Ur but was not to end in Haran. It would not, however, even end in Canaan, for as much as God intended for them to see the land of the promise, the promise was bigger than the land. The promise is about far more than a place, it is about more than a single nation of people of whom they will be the direct ancestors. It is, ultimately, about a promise that will embrace all the peoples of the earth.

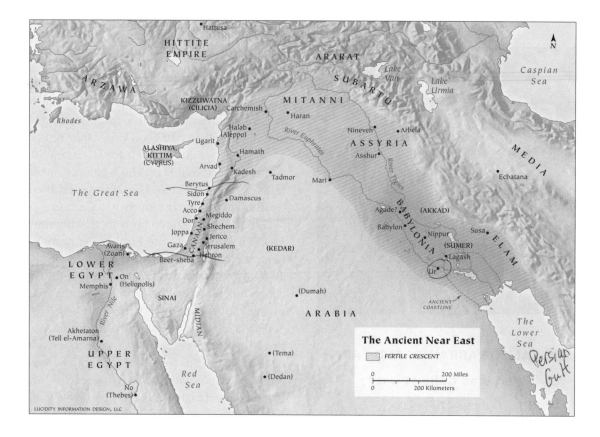

The Ancient Near East

FERTILE CRESCENT

0   200 Miles
0   200 Kilometers

LUCIDITY INFORMATION DESIGN, LLC

These pilgrims are from a past so ancient that their story blends indistinguishably with legend. The legendary overtones, however, do not obscure the fact that all who will eventually call upon the one God as God can trace their own call to become pilgrims in faith to Abram's call.

The Journey Begins

Genesis 12:4-5

> 12:4Abram went as the LORD directed him, and Lot went with him. Abram was seventy-five years old when he left Haran. 5Abram took his wife Sarai, his brother's son Lot, all the possessions that they had accumulated, and the persons they had acquired in Haran, and they set out for the land of Canaan.

"Abram went as the LORD directed him" (Gen 12:4). This is the faithful obedience for which people of faith—even differing faiths—have remembered Abram/Abraham in every subsequent generation. Abram, Sarai, and Lot leave the place in which Terah had settled. Terah had put down stakes, perhaps even roots, in Haran. His son, his daughter-in-law, and his grandson from another son resume the journey he had once begun: "Canaan or bust."

Abram may be leaving a home behind and stepping out in faith to Canaan, but he takes all that he has with him. He has a lot of possessions, and they all go with him. Some of his possessions are said to be people.

His wealth and the nature of his possessions might bother us. We are rightly concerned about the ethics of accumulating "persons." But this concern was not shared by those who made certain that his story was handed on to us. This was a vastly different age than ours, and what they meant to tell us about his possessions was an important aspect of his faith, not his ethics.

If we are curious as to just how wealthy Abram is, our suspicions are laid to rest in 13:2. "Now Abram was very rich in livestock, silver and gold." Abram needs a lot of people just to keep his stuff together on the journey!

We might more easily picture him in our own cultural context as a wealthy, retired business baron who has invested everything in a fleet of sleek, luxurious motor homes so that he, his wife, and a slew of faithful household employees (he might have butlers, maids, and cooks, as well as accountants and mechanics, just to name a few) can hit the road without missing any of the comforts of home, even though they now have no place to call home.

Eventually, biblical authors will present us with a different message about wealth and the call of God. Paul reminds the Corinthians that while they are rich in faith in Christ, their humble circumstances are linked to the profound loftiness of their calling. "God chose the lowly and despised of the world, those who count for nothing, to reduce to nothing those who are something, so that no human being might boast before God" (1 Cor 1:28-29).

But something else is being said about Abram. We are to understand that he is a person of importance—a person of significance—and his wealth is a sign of God's favor. It is to Abram's credit that as significant a person as he is, even with all his wealth, he is answering a call that unsettles him. Abram has been called for a purpose larger than himself, toward a future generations beyond what he will ever see.

Even as we take stock of Abram's wealth, stature, and dignity, he will shock us by exposing a very deep flaw in his character. He is unwilling to trust God with something—someone—very important to his calling. In an act of cowardice, Abram betrays Sarai.

The re-naming of **Abram (to Abraham) and Sarai (to Sarah)** takes place in Genesis 17 following the institution of the covenant of circumcision (17:5, 15). Although the meaning of their new names does not change significantly (*Sarai* and *Sarah* both mean "princess," while *Abram* and *Abraham* are two forms of "exalted father"), the name-change indicates a change in their relationship with God and a new share in the blessings God will bestow.

Abram's Lie

Genesis 12:10-20

12:10There was famine in the land; so Abram went down to Egypt to sojourn there, since the famine in the land was severe. 11When he was about to enter Egypt, he said to his wife Sarai: "I know well how beautiful a woman you are. 12When the Egyptians see you, they will say, 'She is his wife'; then they will kill me, but let you live. 13Please say, therefore, that you are my sister, so that it may go well with me on your account and my life may be spared for your sake." 14When Abram came to Egypt, the Egyptians saw how beautiful the woman was; and when Pharaoh's courtiers saw her, 15they praised her to Pharaoh. So she was taken into Pharaoh's palace. 16On her account it went very well with Abram, and he received flocks and herds, male and female slaves, male and female asses, and camels.

17But the LORD struck Pharaoh and his household with severe plagues because of Abram's wife Sarai. 18Then Pharaoh summoned Abram and said to him: "How could you do this to me! Why didn't you tell me she was your wife? 19Why did you say, 'She is my sister,' so that I took her for my wife? Here, then, is your wife. Take her and be gone!"

20Then Pharaoh gave men orders concerning him, and they sent him on his way, with his wife and all that belonged to him.

This is a deep flaw in Abram/Abraham's character, for it is a sin he will repeat when he lets Abimelech, king of Gerar, take Sarah as an object of his desire on the premise that she is Abraham's sister (Gen 20). We naturally have questions about these two accounts. However old Sarai might be when Pharaoh takes her, Sarah herself claims to be withered with age before Abimelech is deceived into believing she is just Abraham's sister. What is his attraction to a ninety-year-old woman? And is she Abraham's sister? He claims she actually is in Genesis 20:12: "She is in truth my sister, but only my father's daughter, not my mother's; and so she became my wife." Sister-brother marriages, while later forbidden in Mosaic law (Lev 18:11), did exist in adjacent cultures of the time. But the genealogy of Terah and Abram we read in Genesis 11:27-30 makes no mention of Sarai being Terah's daughter.

These are matters scholars struggle with, but many good scholars are careful to give the account as we read it back to us as a story we have to deal with on its own terms. The story is making a point about Abram/Abraham that we are meant to notice because we are told it twice. Our hero is not always so heroic. His loyalty to Sarah is more than just suspect, it is faulty at the core, and so it should come as no surprise that his faithfulness to God will itself have to be tested.

Look about You . . .

Genesis 13:7-12, 14-17

^{13:7}There were quarrels between the herdsmen of Abram's livestock and those of Lot's. (At this time the Canaanites and the Perizzites were occupying the land.)

⁸So Abram said to Lot: "Let there be no strife between you and me, or between your herdsmen and mine, for we are kinsmen. ⁹Is not the whole land at your disposal? Please separate from me. If you prefer the left, I will go to the right; if you prefer the right, I will go to the left." ¹⁰Lot looked about and saw how well watered the whole Jordan Plain was as far as Zoar, like the LORD's own garden, or like Egypt. (This was before the LORD had destroyed Sodom and Gomorrah.) ¹¹Lot, therefore, chose for himself the whole Jordan Plain and set out eastward. Thus they separated from each other; ¹²Abram stayed in the land of Canaan, while Lot settled among the cities of the Plain, pitching his tents near Sodom.

¹⁴ After Lot had left, the LORD said to Abram: "Look about you, and from where you are, gaze to the north and south, east and west; ¹⁵all the land that you see I will give to you and your descendants forever. ¹⁶I will make your descendants like the dust of the earth; if anyone could count the dust of the earth, your descendants too might be counted. ¹⁷Set forth and walk about in the land, through its length and breadth, for to you I will give it."

Abram and Lot, uncle and nephew, go their separate ways in order to honor their close relationship. Those who tend their large herds have begun arguing. If disputes went any further it might lead to contention within their family. Abram is generous toward his nephew. He tells him that the choice of land is Lot's; Abram will not choose, he will merely take what is left him.

Lot makes his choice wisely, at least it would seem so at the time. He sees a stretch of land watered and flourishing like the original Garden of Eden and says, "I'll take that." Lot leaves with his herds and Abram accepts his fate. He had put his future out of his own hands and left his destiny for Lot to decide, but that actually only put it into the hands of the Almighty.

"Look about you," God tells him. And as he looks he hears God's promise resounding in his ears. The land in every direction, as far as the eye can see, will be his and his descendants'. And his descendants will be uncountable. This is Abram's destiny.

Actually, it is his descendants' destiny.

Which would have been harder to believe, that all this was his, or that it would belong to his innumerable offspring? As we will see later, Abram will come to possess very little of the land himself. He will live his life as an alien in the land that he knows is a gift by faith, a gift waiting a time long past his own. He is, however, to walk about its length and breadth, believing all the while in the promise. But for now, he must mostly wait for a descendant with whom he can confide the promise.

Abram's Faith

Genesis 15:1-6

> [15:1]Some time after these events, this word of the LORD came to Abram in a vision:
>
> "Fear not, Abram!
>   I am your shield;
>   I will make your reward very great."
>
> [2]But Abram said, "O Lord GOD, what good will your gifts be, if I keep on being childless and have as my heir the steward of my house, Eliezer?" [3]Abram continued, "See, you have given me no offspring, and so one of my servants will be my heir." [4]Then the word of the LORD came to him: "No, that one shall not be your heir; your own issue shall be your heir." [5]He took him outside and said: "Look up at the sky and count the stars, if you can. Just so," he added, "shall your descendants be." [6]Abram put his faith in the LORD, who credited it to him as an act of righteousness.

Once again, God comes to Abram and assures him of a magnificent future. And Abram responds, in not so many words, with "Enough already with your promises!"

Abram has answered God's call. He and Sarai have left Haran far behind and have entered Canaan just as God had directed them. *But what good are these promises?* Abram asks. *I have no child.* In English we miss the sarcastic way Abram addresses God in Hebrew. Abram complains that he has no son to inherit the promises except for a house steward from Damascus. What is translated as "the steward of my house" is, in Hebrew, the coupling of the word for son with the last three consonants found in Damascus. Had he said it in English it would sound something like, "I have no son but my son-mascus from Damascus!"

Such punning from Abram would sound quite daring, if not downright flippant, tossed as freely as it is into the Almighty's ear. Abram is not just tired of waiting for the promise; he is reminding God that time is running out.

God does not bend to Abram's impatience. What God has said will come to pass will surely do so. God challenges Abram to count the stars. If he can do that, then maybe he will be able to count his descendants, they will be so many. The promise remains a promise, but it is God who has spoken and so it will be. Abram, for all his impatience—even knowing that time itself is ruling out the possibility of an heir—hears the word God speaks and believes. All the evidence in the world suggests Abram should despair, but his faith is in God, not in any evidence.

Abram's faith is credited to him by God as an act of righteousness.

If you ask St. Paul, this is the most important act of faith in biblical history prior to the act of faith that prompts the cry, "He is risen!" Abram, who is waiting for God to bring about the promise of an heir to the land that is also, as yet, only a promise, believes God will bring it about and is declared righteous for his faith.

Paul carefully examines the circumstances under which Abram makes his act of faith, and notes that Abram was declared righteous while as yet uncircumcised (Rom 4:1-13). Because of that simple fact, Paul proclaims, we can be certain that God accepts uncircumcised Gentiles when they too profess faith. Circumcision is not the way for a Gentile to be declared righteous; that happens when we believe God has raised Jesus Christ from the dead.

Jesus is a direct descendant of Abraham. There are two different genealogies in the Bible tracing Jesus' ancestry directly to him (Matt 1:1-17; Luke 3:23-38). There are three major monotheistic faiths on the planet. Most Jews as well as Arabic Muslims claim a blood connection in their relation to Abraham. Most Christians cannot make the same claim. Instead, we have Paul's assertion that our profession of faith in Jesus as the risen Lord assures us that we, like Abraham, will receive God's declaration of righteousness. We honor Abraham as our ancestor in faith; we don't rely on a personal genealogy to see our connection to him.

Abram's journey of faith has so far only given him a glimpse of what is promised him. He has to believe in the promise or he literally has nothing to show for his faith. This is where Paul's interpretation of Abraham's faith being the precursor of Christian faith is so apt, for, as Paul says to the Corinthians:

> For if the dead are not raised, neither has Christ been raised, and if Christ has not been raised, your faith is vain; you are still in your sins. Then those who have fallen asleep in Christ have perished. If for this life only we have hoped in Christ, we are the most pitiable people of all. (1 Cor 15:16-19)

The pilgrimage of Christian faith is one that extends even beyond this life, embracing in faith the hope of the resurrection. Having this faith teaches us to see everything in this life differently. Because of this faith we have become lifelong pilgrims. Without it, we could only see what is in front of our eyes and our journey would more likely be toward some *thing* rather than toward some *one*.

Abraham's faith, which Paul sets as the model for ours, is also an *act* of faith. It is not simply belief, it is *faith*, and faith expresses itself through *faithfulness*. Abraham's faith will be tested. Does he really have faith? This will only be answered by whether or not he proves to be faithful. But that test will await the fulfillment of God's first promise to Abram; he will have an heir!

 Prayer Starter: It will happen in your life also: those barren moments with no birth in sight. Let Abraham be your mentor in these times. Follow him out under the stars. Gaze at the heavens and offer to God a faith you cannot see or feel.

Hagar and Ishmael

Genesis 16:1-16

16:1Abram's wife Sarai had borne him no children. She had, however, an Egyptian maidservant named Hagar. 2Sarai said to Abram: "The LORD has kept me from bearing children. Have intercourse, then, with my maid; perhaps I shall have sons through her." Abram heeded Sarai's request. 3Thus, after Abram had lived ten years in the land of Canaan, his wife Sarai took her maid, Hagar the Egyptian, and gave her to her husband Abram to be his concubine. 4He had intercourse with her, and she became pregnant. When she became aware of her pregnancy, she looked on her mistress with disdain. 5So Sarai said to Abram: "You are responsible for this outrage against me. I myself gave my maid to your embrace; but ever since she became aware of her pregnancy, she has been looking on me with disdain. May the LORD decide between you and me!" 6Abram told Sarai: "Your maid is in your power. Do to her whatever you please." Sarai then abused her so much that Hagar ran away from her.

7The LORD's messenger found her by a spring in the wilderness, the spring on the road to Shur, 8and he asked, "Hagar, maid of Sarai, where have you come from and where are you going?" She answered, "I am running away from my mistress, Sarai." 9But the LORD's messenger told her: "Go back to your mistress and submit to her abusive treatment. 10I will make your descendants so numerous," added the LORD's messenger, "that they will be too many to count. 11Besides," the LORD's messenger said to her:

> "You are now pregnant and shall bear a son;
> you shall name him Ishmael,
> For the LORD has heard you,
> God has answered you.
> 12He shall be a wild ass of a man,
> his hand against everyone,
> and everyone's hand against him;
> In opposition to all his kin
> shall he encamp."

continue

> ¹³To the LORD who spoke to her she gave a name, saying, "You are the God of Vision"; she meant, "Have I really seen God and remained alive after my vision?" ¹⁴That is why the well is called Beer-lahai-roi. It is between Kadesh and Bered.
>
> ¹⁵Hagar bore Abram a son, and Abram named the son whom Hagar bore him Ishmael. ¹⁶Abram was eighty-six years old when Hagar bore him Ishmael.

The adage, "Be careful what you wish for, you just might get it," is quite appropriate here. Sarai knows well the promise God has made Abram and devises her own plan to make it come about. She gives her maid (her slave) to her husband and tells him to have relations with her. It would seem that she is hopeful that Hagar will become pregnant and bear a son. Indeed, she seems to hope that Abram will have more than one son through Hagar, who is now referred to as Abram's concubine.

Times were different then, to be sure. Even in the biblical world, a wealthy man would often have as many women as he could support without any trace of overt criticism. Today, a wife who would provide a mistress for her husband is the stuff made for more than one racy television series. Many Bible readers would not be amused, however. But there is something beneath the surface in this biblical account that warns us against making Sarai's choice a model for married behavior. It all backfires on Sarai and things get even worse for her maid, Hagar.

Sarai does get exactly what she wishes; Hagar bears a son. The concubine is fruitful and lets the barren wife know it with insufferable pride and disdain. Furious, Sarai, as first wife, demands justice from Abram who delivers the mother of his son into the jealous grip of Sarai. "Do to her whatever you please" (16:6). Tormented beyond endurance, Hagar runs away with her son.

From our vantage, it seems strange that God would send the unfortunate Hagar back to her jealous, punishing mistress. But there is more to this story than is told in the Bible. Here in Genesis, God promises a special providential care for Hagar's son, his future is assured of greatness, and with this promise, Hagar will bear her own future under the harsh hand of her mistress with hope, no matter what the future brings to her personally.

Hagar has entered her own pilgrimage. No matter how long or how far she journeys with these other pilgrims, she is on her own journey of faith now, trusting God for her son and his own unique future.

Far beyond what is allotted him in the words of Genesis, Hagar's son Ishmael will be regarded in Islam as the true child of promise. If we are to believe in God's providential care for Hagar and her offspring as reported to us in our Scripture, then we too must marvel at the greatness of Ishmael's heritage.

 It was **a widely accepted custom** in the ancient world for a wife who was barren to provide a slave woman as a concubine for her husband so that the continuance of his line would be ensured. Evidence for this practice can be found in Old Assyrian marriage contracts as well as in the Nuzi texts (stone tablets dating from the fourteenth century BC, discovered in northern Iraq). While the laws of neighboring cultures *required* wives who were infertile to provide the means for their husbands to insure their posterity, it is important to note that Sarai herself freely suggests this course of action to Abram.

A Change of Identity

Genesis 17:1-8, 15

> ¹⁷:¹When Abram was ninety-nine years old, the LORD appeared to him and said: "I am God the Almighty. Walk in my presence and be blameless.
>
> *continue*

²Between you and me I will establish my covenant, and I will multiply you exceedingly."

³When Abram prostrated himself, God continued to speak to him: ⁴"My covenant with you is this: you are to become the father of a host of nations. ⁵No longer shall you be called Abram; your name shall be Abraham, for I am making you the father of a host of nations. ⁶I will render you exceedingly fertile; I will make nations of you; kings shall stem from you. ⁷I will maintain my covenant with you and your descendants after you throughout the ages as an everlasting pact, to be your God and the God of your descendants after you. ⁸I will give to you and to your descendants after you the land in which you are now staying, the whole land of Canaan, as a permanent possession; and I will be their God." . . .

¹⁵God further said to Abraham: "As for your wife Sarai, do not call her Sarai; her name shall be Sarah."

One of the first things many people notice about God's call to Abraham and Sarah to leave their homeland, is that they are not yet "Abraham" and "Sarah." At this early stage in the narrative (though they are already mature in years), they are called "Abram" and "Sarai." When Abram receives the call in Genesis 12:1, he is seventy-five. When he is ninety-nine and has still not encountered all that the journey will ask of him, God makes a special covenant with him, the covenant of circumcision (17:10). "No longer shall you be called Abram," God tells him, "your name shall be Abraham" (17:5). In the same appearance, God goes on to tell the newly named Abraham, "As for your wife Sarai, do not call her Sarai; her name shall be Sarah" (17:15).

Answering God's call and responding in faith has given the couple a new identity before God. It is not that the meaning of their names have significantly changed; they haven't. But any change of name marks some change in identity. This change in identity is because they have been brought into a new, special, covenanted relationship with their God.

For Abraham, this new identity is something he can see and, for the immediate future anyway, feel. Abraham has been marked with change in the most personal, physical area of his identity as a man. But Sarah too will see changes. She will bear a child in her advanced age, the offspring through whom God promises them that their descendants will become more numerous than the stars of the heavens, even more than the sands of the seashore (Gen 22:17).

Not unlike the new name God gave Abram and Sarai, our names provide us with an identity. By the time we are adults, we have probably made so many personal associations with our name that we seldom bother to think about it. It's just who we are, this name by which our peers call us. But just like Abraham and Sarah, our name is a calling. When our parents and loved ones first started speaking to us, they probably started calling us by name. It is by the sound of that name that we were first called into relationship with other human beings. Our name is what drew our earliest attention to other voices and held our attention on their gaze as they brought us into the discovery that we belong to and with others in a bond of love. This calling was probably deeply enriched by warm, loving hugs and kisses as well.

The power of our name as a calling into relationship is magnified and transformed through the sacrament of baptism. Through the waters of baptism, we are called by name into a new relationship with God, a covenant sealed in the blood of Christ, which baptism both symbolizes and effects in a special way (see Col 2:12). Our name, in baptism, is made a Christian name even if it is not commonly known as a saint's name. Our baptismal name is our calling to become followers of Christ.

Through the gift of a name, and by the grace of baptism, we have become pilgrim people. We are called by God into an adventure of faith that extends the promise of being united with the one to whom we are called (Christ) at the end of our pilgrimage. God promises to be with us on the journey and to meet us as its end and goal. Nothing else is promised us. To be a pilgrim requires faith; it would be a very scary journey without it.

God's Pilgrimage of Friendship

Genesis 18:17-22

> [18:17]The LORD reflected: "Shall I hide from Abraham what I am about to do, [18]now that he is to become a great and populous nation, and all the nations of the earth are to find blessing in him? [19]Indeed, I have singled him out that he may direct his sons and his posterity to keep the way of the LORD by doing what is right and just, so that the LORD may carry into effect for Abraham the promises he made about him." [20]Then the LORD said: "The outcry against Sodom and Gomorrah is so great, and their sin so grave, [21]that I must go down and see whether or not their actions fully correspond to the cry against them that comes to me. I mean to find out."
>
> [22]While the two men walked on farther toward Sodom, the LORD remained standing before Abraham.

In 2 Chronicles 20:7, Isaiah 41:8, and again in James 2:23, Abraham is referred to as God's friend. Little wonder, then, that God would not keep the plans for Sodom and Gomorrah secret from him. Abraham, in turn, will not keep his peace in God's presence. The account above goes on at great length with Abraham pestering God with an ever-narrowing concern that Sodom might be spared judgment if there should be some righteous souls dwelling there (Gen 18:23-33). Abraham begins with fifty: "Suppose there were fifty innocent people in the city; would you wipe out the place, rather than spare it for the sake of the fifty innocent people within it?"

God assures his friend Abraham that if fifty righteous are found in the city, it will not be destroyed. And so Abraham ventures to dare ask God if Sodom would be destroyed if there were only forty-five, and God answers, "I will not destroy it, if I find forty-five there." Time and again Abraham goes on, asking what the city's fate would be if there were but forty righteous, then thirty, then twenty, and finally ten. Each time, God assures him if that many righteous are found in the city, then for the sake of the righteous, the guilty would be spared. Unfortunately, not even ten are found. There is even room for questioning whether Lot and his family are spared because they are righteous or simply because of their kinship to Abraham.

Abraham's intercession on behalf of any righteous that might be dwelling in Sodom often overshadows other significant details in this account. Just prior to this, God has come down from heaven and visited Abraham, promising him that in a year's time he and Sarah will be parents to a son. Let us focus our attention here on the fact that the Lord comes down from heaven because Abraham is God's friend. God will make this friend privy to the divine council. The friend can, in fact, influence God's decision making.

Abraham is the one we usually think of as a pilgrim. But in this account, it is God who is on pilgrimage. True, God is described here in terms that are called anthropomorphic—God is described as if he were a man of flesh and blood who must leave his heaven and venture forth upon the earth in order to investigate what horrors these human creatures are fomenting.

This caricature should not diminish God in our eyes, however. It tells us that God wants to be involved. God does not sit idly by and wait for our evil to become so rampant that none can be saved. Even more important, though, is that God first visits a friend. Is it just to clue Abraham in? Friends, after all, tell their friends what they are doing. But this God is willing to wander the earth in search for a friend before imposing judgment. The Divine Pilgrim listens patiently to the friend's fears and concerns.

Surely our God has friends who care enough for the earth to plead for patience from the Almighty. Our pilgrim God is looking for us! Are there enough friends of God here to spare the world?

The question might also be asked, did Abraham have to stop counting down at ten?

The Child of Promise

Genesis 21:1-3

21:1The LORD took note of Sarah as he had said he would; he did for her as he had promised. 2Sarah became pregnant and bore Abraham a son in his old age, at the set time that God had stated. 3Abraham gave the name Isaac to this son of his whom Sarah bore him.

Sarah bears a son, Isaac, just as God had promised she would and at the time God had stated. These verses are presented to us as a sure testimony to God's faithfulness. In the abundance of God's faithfulness, Abraham is told that Ishmael will also become a great nation. "As for the son of the slave woman, I will make a great nation of him also, since he too is your offspring" (Gen 21:13).

The Testing of Abraham

Genesis 22:1-3

22:1Some time after these events, God put Abraham to the test. He called to him, "Abraham!" "Ready!" he replied. 2Then God said: "Take your son Isaac, your only one, whom you love, and go to the land of Moriah. There you shall offer him up as a holocaust on a height that I will point out to you." 3Early the next morning Abraham saddled his donkey, took with him his son Isaac, and two of his servants as well, and with the wood that he had cut for the holocaust, set out for the place of which God had told him.

This testing of Abraham is an amazing example of powerful story-telling, but it gives many of us the "willies" as an account of God's activity!

Within the context of the story, however, God needs to see just how loyal Abraham is. The testing of Abraham is somewhat like the testing of Job. In the book of Job, the Satan (depicted there as a member of God's heavenly court) warns God that Job is only a good man because God has so richly rewarded him. Take away Job's blessings and Job will end up cursing God.

Perhaps there is a question here in Genesis about whether the promises God has made to Abraham are too great. Abraham has been faithful in that he has believed the promises, but has Abraham perhaps been faithful because of the promises? If God took away the promise, would Abraham still be faithful?

After all, no one else has ever been this faithful before, not even Noah, and it is not as if Abraham is utterly without flaws. Remember how he lied about his relationship to Sarah and how he was willing to prostitute her for his own safety and well-being (Gen 12:11-20; 20:1-2)?

So God is putting Abraham to the test.

Considered in the abstract, this is a conundrum. Whatever Abraham does will result in catastrophe. Either the promise of an heir through Sarah will not have been fulfilled after all or God will now have evidence that Abraham is unfaithful and unworthy of the promise. What God is asking is not only against reason but also against God's own promise, but because God has asked it, Abraham must act as directed, and so he does.

We want to protest this. God does not ask for human sacrifice! Therefore, God would not ask Abraham to do this, and so, if it were you or I being told by a voice from the heavens to sacrifice our child, we should answer, "Go away you demon from hell! May God rebuke you!"

But this is God asking, which is a conundrum for us as well as Abraham. We want Abraham to do the right thing, which on no account means taking a knife to his child. The story will not change, however. And so we must follow Abraham and Isaac to the hill of sacrifice, watching all the while as Isaac dutifully carries the branches that are to kindle his own holocaust.

The Faithfulness of Abraham

Genesis 22:4-18

²²:⁴On the third day Abraham got sight of the place from afar. ⁵Then he said to his servants: "Both of you stay here with the donkey, while the boy and I go on over yonder. We will worship and then come back to you." ⁶Thereupon Abraham took the wood for the holocaust and laid it on his son Isaac's shoulders, while he himself carried the fire and the knife. ⁷As the two walked on together, Isaac spoke to his father Abraham. "Father!" he said. "Yes, son," he replied. Isaac continued, "Here are the fire and the wood, but where is the sheep for the holocaust?" ⁸"Son," Abraham answered, "God himself will provide the sheep for the holocaust." Then the two continued going forward.

⁹When they came to the place of which God had told him, Abraham built an altar there and arranged the wood on it. Next he tied up his son Isaac, and put him on top of the wood on the altar. ¹⁰Then he reached out and took the knife to slaughter his son. ¹¹But the LORD's messenger called to him from heaven, "Abraham, Abraham!" "Yes, Lord," he answered. ¹²"Do not lay your hand on the boy," said the messenger. "Do not do the least thing to him. I know now how devoted you are to God, since you did not withhold from me your own beloved son." ¹³As Abraham looked about, he spied a ram caught by its horns in the thicket. So he went and took the ram and offered it up as a holocaust in place of his son. ¹⁴Abraham named the site Yahweh-yireh; hence people now say, "On the mountain the LORD will see."

¹⁵Again the LORD's messenger called to Abraham from heaven ¹⁶and said: "I swear by myself, declares the LORD, that because you acted as you did in not withholding from me your beloved son, ¹⁷I will bless you abundantly and make your descendants as countless as the stars of the sky and the sands of the seashore; your descendants shall take possession of the gates of their enemies, ¹⁸and in your descendants all the nations of the earth shall find blessing—all this because you obeyed my command."

The event that saves Isaac also miraculously delivers the story from being a horrible tale about God. At its very climax, we learn that God knows all along what God will do; the Almighty just didn't know what Abraham would do.

Much in Christian theology responds that this cannot be so. God knows all things and knew from the beginning of time that Abraham would be faithful even in this most unthinkable of circumstances. And so it might be theologically more correct to believe that it was for Abraham's own sake that he was put to the test. It was Abraham who needed to know that in spite of his flawed character the God who called him to faithfulness is able to strengthen him in faithfulness. The story itself, however, makes no such suggestion.

This story does have something to tell us. Pilgrims as we are in life, not everything we experience on our way will make sense. Tragedies never will, and through whatever dark places we must pass, if we are to persevere in hope, we must still prove ourselves faithful, even when God asks too much of us, takes too much from us. God's promises are not forgotten. God has not forgotten us.

The Cave of Machpelah

Genesis 23:1-20

23:1The span of Sarah's life was one hundred and twenty-seven years. 2She died in Kiriatharba (that is, Hebron) in the land of Canaan, and Abraham performed the customary mourning rites for her. 3Then he left the side of his dead one and addressed the Hittites: 4"Although I am a resident alien among you, sell me from your holdings a piece of property for a burial ground, that I may bury my dead wife." 5The Hittites answered Abraham: "Please, sir, 6listen to us! You are an elect of God among us. Bury your dead in the choicest of our burial sites. None of us would deny you his burial ground for the burial of your dead." 7Abraham, however, began to bow low before the local citizens, the Hittites, 8while he appealed to them: "If you will allow me room for burial of my dead, listen to me! Intercede for me with Ephron, son of Zohar, asking him 9to sell me the cave of Machpelah that he owns; it is at the edge of his field. Let him sell it to me in your presence, at its full price, for a burial place."

10Now Ephron was present with the Hittites. So Ephron the Hittite replied to Abraham in the hearing of the Hittites who sat on his town council: 11"Please, sir, listen to me! I give you both the field and the cave in it; in the presence of my kinsmen I make this gift. Bury your dead!" 12But Abraham, after bowing low before the local citizens, addressed Ephron in the hearing of these men: 13"Ah, if only you would please listen to me! I will pay you the price of the field. Accept it from me, that I may bury my dead there." 14Ephron replied to Abraham, "Please, 15sir, listen to me! A piece of land worth four hundred shekels of silver— what is that between you and me, as long as you can bury your dead?" 16Abraham accepted Ephron's terms; he weighed out to him the silver that Ephron had stipulated in the hearing of the Hittites, four hundred shekels of silver at the current market value.

17Thus Ephron's field in Machpelah, facing Mamre, together with its cave and all the trees anywhere within its limits, was conveyed 18to Abraham by purchase in the presence of all the Hittites who sat on Ephron's town council. 19After this transaction, Abraham buried his wife Sarah in the cave of the field of Machpelah, facing Mamre (that is, Hebron) in the land of Canaan. 20Thus the field with its cave was transferred from the Hittites to Abraham as a burial place.

All journeys come to an end.

Our ears should not be tricked into thinking that Ephron the Hittite is offering Abraham a gravesite for Sarah free of charge. The protests against payment are simply niceties of the time that surround some very shrewd bargaining. Besides, Abraham must have the equivalent of a deed. A gift of a burial site might be regarded simply as an accommodation to a need. The whole point is that Abraham is now a landowner in Canaan. The first smidgeon of Canaan, which God has promised in its entirety to Abraham and his descendants, is now Abraham's, free and clear.

The two promises, one of innumerable offspring and the other of all the land that his eyes could see, have both now received tangible down payments. Isaac is now a young man and Abraham owns real estate in Canaan. It is a grave, and when he dies his bones will be placed there beside Sarah's (Gen 25:7-10).

Just Isaac and a cave in Hebron? Is this the full extent to which God's promises to Abraham were fulfilled in his lifetime? It was either very little or everything, depending on whether Abraham's faith in the One who made the promise was well placed or not. Abraham's faith made him a pilgrim throughout his life and it seems that was no different at his death. He would have had to look beyond the evidence of his senses and trust instead in the God who made the promises.

It is an affirmation of our faith that the Creator of all, the one, the only God, was Abraham's God. Did Abraham truly understand that there was no other god than the God who had called him?

God did not call Abraham and Sarah because they were theologians. God did call them to be faithful and Scripture records that they were. Whatever possible pantheon Abraham might have chosen from, it was only to this one God that he was faithful. In generations to come, Abraham's faith in God will help Israel identify just who their God is: "I am the God of Abraham." This will remain true even for Jesus and Peter in the New Testament (Matt 22:32; Acts 3:13).

There was much that Abraham did not understand, least of all the actual scope of the promise he had received. Abraham's personal understanding of death probably did not go beyond the realization that his flesh would return to dust and his bones would fall into a disheveled pile on the floor of a cave. What he didn't understand was, nevertheless, at the heart of God's promises to Abraham.

When Jesus scolds those who doubt the resurrection of the dead, he reminds them of who God is. "Have you not read what was said to you by God, 'I am the God of Abraham, the God of Isaac, and the God of Jacob'? He is not the God of the dead but of the living" (Matt 22:31b-32). In this most subtle of ways, Abraham's faith becomes the first proclamation of the Easter gospel, and the open door to all the peoples of the world to embrace his God as ours.

Because we are called to a faith like Abraham's and Sarah's, we know that to live our lives in faith is to identify ourselves as sojourners in an alien land; our true home is something greater than can be touched or walked upon.

Hebron and the shrine of Machpelah

EXPLORING LESSON ONE

1. When he is called to leave Haran and journey to a land that God "will show [him]" (Gen 12:1), Abram takes along "all the possessions" he has acquired (Gen 12:5). Why might this detail concerning what Abram takes with him into Canaan be noteworthy?

_____

_____

_____

_____

2. a) Why does Abram/Abraham lie about his relationship to his wife, first to Pharaoh (Gen 12:10-20) and then to Abimelech, King of Gerar (Gen 20)? What do these lies tell you about Abraham?

_____

_____

_____

   b) Without defending Abraham's actions, can you imagine circumstances where people might do desperate things if they feel threatened and isolated in new surroundings? How does this perspective affect your understanding of the text?

_____

_____

_____

3. In what ways does the story of Abraham invite us to consider the relationship between *faith* (our belief in the promises of God) and *faithfulness* (the expression of our faith through action)?

_____

_____

_____

_____

4. According to Paul, how can Christians claim Abraham as an ancestor (Rom 9:7-8; Gal 3:7, 29)? In what way does this claim differ from the Abrahamic ancestry of Jews and Arabic Muslims?

_____

_____

_____

_____

5. a) Sarai seeks to anticipate God's promise of an heir by giving her maid Hagar to her husband so that she might "have sons through her" (Gen 16:2). Do her actions fulfill God's plan?

_____

_____

_____

_____

   b) Can you think of times in your life when you grew impatient for God's plan to unfold and tried to take matters into your own hands? What lessons did you learn through those experiences?

_____

_____

_____

_____

6. Compare and contrast the promises God makes to Hagar (Gen 16:7-16) with those he had made earlier to Abraham (Gen 12:1-3; 15:1-6). What similarities and differences do you notice?

_____

_____

_____

_____

7. a) Naming—the authority to grant or change a name—is a notable theme throughout Scripture (e.g., Gen 2:19-20; 35:10; Matt 16:17-18; Luke 1:13, 31). What is the significance of the changes in Abram's and Sarai's names proclaimed by God in Genesis 17:1-8, 15?

_____

_____

_____

_____

   b) Has a change in name marked you as a pilgrim? Examples might include name changes at confirmation, marriage or religious vows, or even new nicknames or titles.

_____

_____

_____

_____

8. What does the visit that God pays to Abraham in Genesis 18 reveal about the nature of God and his relationship with those who are his "friends"?

_____

_____

_____

_____

9. What lessons for your own life can you draw from the story of God's testing of Abraham in Genesis 22:1-12?

_____

_____

_____

_____

10. What is the importance of Abraham's purchase of property in Canaan for the burial of Sarah (Gen 23:1-20)?

_____

_____

_____

_____

CLOSING PRAYER

Prayer

Again the Lord's *messenger called to Abraham from heaven and said:"I swear by myself, declares the* Lord, *that because you acted as you did in not withholding from me your beloved son, I will bless you abundantly and make your descendants as countless as the stars of the sky and the sands of the seashore; your descendants shall take possession of the gates of their enemies, and in your descendants all the nations of the earth shall find blessing—all this because you obeyed my command."*   (Gen 22:15-18)

Heavenly Father, you rewarded the faithfulness of Abraham by confirming the promises made to him at the very start of his pilgrimage. May we also be faithful, and at the end of our earthly pilgrimage, may we realize the promise of salvation through your son, Jesus Christ. Strengthen our faith and grant assurance of your love and friendship to all believers, especially those we pray for today . . .

LESSON TWO

Exodus and Entry

Begin your personal study and group discussion with a simple and sincere prayer such as:

Prayer

God, you are the source and goal of all life. Strengthen, support, and guide us on our earthly pilgrimage so that, nourished by your word and inspired by your Son's example, we may persevere in faith until we find ourselves home at last in your heavenly kingdom.

Read pages 32–44, Lesson Two.

Respond to the questions on pages 45–47, Exploring Lesson Two.

The Closing Prayer on page 48 is for your personal use and may be used at the end of group discussion.

EXODUS AND ENTRY

A Basket among the Reeds

Exodus 1:12b–2:10

¹:¹²ᵇThe Egyptians, then, dreaded the Israelites ¹³and reduced them to cruel slavery, ¹⁴making life bitter for them with hard work in mortar and brick and all kinds of field work—the whole cruel fate of slaves.

¹⁵The king of Egypt told the Hebrew midwives, one of whom was called Shiphrah and the other Puah, ¹⁶"When you act as midwives for the Hebrew women and see them giving birth, if it is a boy, kill him; but if it is a girl, she may live." ¹⁷The midwives, however, feared God; they did not do as the king of Egypt had ordered them, but let the boys live. ¹⁸So the king summoned the midwives and asked them, "Why have you acted thus, allowing the boys to live?" ¹⁹The midwives answered Pharaoh, "The Hebrew women are not like the Egyptian women. They are robust and give birth before the midwife arrives." ²⁰Therefore God dealt well with the midwives. The people, too, increased and grew strong. ²¹And because the midwives feared God, he built up families for them. ²²Pharaoh then commanded all his subjects, "Throw into the river every boy that is born to the Hebrews, but you may let all the girls live."

²:¹Now a certain man of the house of Levi married a Levite woman, ²who conceived and bore a son. Seeing that he was a goodly child, she hid him for three months. ³When she could hide him no longer, she took a papyrus basket, daubed it with bitumen and pitch, and putting the child in it, placed it among the reeds on the river bank. ⁴His sister stationed herself at a distance to find out what would happen to him.

⁵Pharaoh's daughter came down to the river to bathe, while her maids walked along the river bank. Noticing the basket among the reeds, she sent her handmaid to fetch it. ⁶On opening it, she looked, and lo, there was a baby boy, crying! She was moved with pity for him and said, "It is one of the Hebrews' children." ⁷Then his sister asked Pharaoh's daughter, "Shall I go and call one of the

Hebrew women to nurse the child for you?" ⁸"Yes, do so," she answered. So the maiden went and called the child's own mother. ⁹Pharaoh's daughter said to her, "Take this child and nurse it for me, and I will repay you." The woman therefore took the child and nursed it. ¹⁰When the child grew, she brought him to Pharaoh's daughter, who adopted him as her son and called him Moses; for she said, "I drew him out of the water."

Birth is an unprecedented pilgrimage for each of us. We enter life by passing from darkness to light, emerging from a warm, wet world of near perfect physical communion with a mother only to be jarred by glaring lights, loud noises, and the unfamiliarity of dry air. Wrapped usually in a cloth, arms enfold us and our journey begins. We have entered the world, but there is almost nothing we can do on our own except breathe and eagerly accept the nourishment given us. Yet every gesture we make, every attempt at rolling over, will help hone skills leading toward the independence of crawling and ultimately walking on our own. The journey of faith, however, is one that often takes shape in our hearts and minds even more gradually.

Moses' pilgrimage of faith—one of the most significant of all time—truly begins with his birth. At his birth Moses inherits the perilous status of a persecuted minority. God's people, the descendants promised to Abraham, have been enslaved in Egypt for four hundred years (Gen 15:13; Exod 12:40). Now, all Hebrew males are ordered to be drowned at birth.

Moses is put into the river, but not to drown. To save his life, he is pushed into the waters inside a basket prepared with the same care as Noah's ark (Gen 6:14). With no more than a push from his mother's hand, the hand of divine providence, seemingly hidden for four centuries, begins to reveal itself as the mighty hand of liberation.

Who can believe the bravery and creativity of the **midwives to the Hebrews**? They not only defy the orders of the king but they outwit him as well. Surely they were aware that a man of the time and of his rank would never have witnessed a birth and could not possibly dispute their description of robust (and speedy) births. What's the reason for their disobedience to the king? They "feared God" (Exod 1:17, 21). And in spite of the possibility that they were not themselves Hebrew, their allegiance was foremost to God and to the ways of God, not to Pharaoh and his ways. Their courage was a natural consequence of knowing God. Their obedience to God, the author of life, prevented them from participating in bringing about death. Siphrah and Puah, appearing here before the Mosaic covenant has been made, nonetheless live the covenant values of mercy, steadfast love, and justice. They embody and prefigure covenant living whether they know it or not. And they remind even modern readers that a basic reverence for God results in good fruit.

Pharaoh's evil intent toward the Hebrews is born of an all-too-familiar prejudice. The Hebrew people were originally immigrants and they were welcomed in Egypt because their presence brought prosperity to the land (Gen 47:1-6, 23-27). When their numbers increased, however, they were seen as a threat (Exod 1:8-10). Observing the situation through the inspired eye of the Bible, we are able to see the irony in Pharaoh's attempt to resolve the "Hebrew problem" through infanticide. Pharaoh's ruthlessly calculated plan to drown all the male children not only results in their great liberator being raised as one of Pharaoh's own family but also returns Moses to intimate contact with his real mother and his Hebrew family.

Moses' Hebrew family also belongs to the tribe of Levi, descended from one of the twelve sons of Jacob (Gen 35:22-26). The importance of this at Moses' birth poses a question like that of "which came first, the chicken or the egg?" Moses' birth into this family either establishes the tribe of Levi as the source of Israel's priests, or, just as likely, his being a Levite legitimates Moses and his brother Aaron for the roles they are about to play in Israel's salvation history.

Moses Flees to Midian

Exodus 2:11-15a

2:11On one occasion, after Moses had grown up, when he visited his kinsmen and witnessed their forced labor, he saw an Egyptian striking a Hebrew, one of his own kinsmen. 12Looking about and seeing no one, he slew the Egyptian and hid him in the sand. 13The next day he went out again, and now two Hebrews were fighting! So he asked the culprit, "Why are you striking your fellow Hebrew?" 14But he replied, "Who has appointed you ruler and judge over us? Are you thinking of killing me as you killed the Egyptian?" Then Moses became afraid and thought, "The affair must certainly be known."

15Pharaoh, too, heard of the affair and sought to put him to death. But Moses fled from him and stayed in the land of Midian.

Written long before any literature that describes psychological turmoil, Exodus nevertheless hands us a dramatic situation that reveals Moses' loyalties while also casting a shadow over his character. Moses has become a man, but what kind of man? As a child, he enjoyed intimate contact with his family of birth, but he is also the adopted child of Pharaoh's daughter. During the influential years of adolescence and early adulthood, he enjoyed privilege, power, and luxuries beyond imagination for a Hebrew. This would be heady stuff for a young man to resist. Would the disparity between the two lifestyles have eaten at Moses over the years? Perhaps he just felt extremely lucky or blessed. Maybe he would even tell himself that there must have been something in him that made him worthy of his good fortune. We don't get to see inside Moses; what is inside him is revealed by his actions.

While his moral character may not be fully formed when he returns from a visit with his poor, enslaved kinsmen, his response at seeing another Hebrew beaten by an Egyptian determines his loyalties in a flash. He looks about for possible witnesses to an act he has already settled on in his heart and strikes out murderously at the Egyptian attacker.

We don't read a verdict on Moses' action, but he naturally fears retribution by the Egyptians. But how should we regard him? Was he a revolutionary in a just cause, or did he murder in hot blood? During the early days of the American Revolution, peace-loving citizens might have found it just as hard to judge the character of those who later would be declared heroes. It will take more than this event to turn Moses into a real hero, however. Guilty or innocent, God is nowhere near finished with Moses.

And so our hero flees the scene, and this flight will prove to be a major step in his pilgrimage, though he probably only sees it as an escape.

I Will Be with You

Exodus 2:23–3:14

2:23A long time passed, during which the king of Egypt died. Still the Israelites groaned and cried out because of their slavery. As their cry for release went up to God, 24he heard their groaning and was mindful of his covenant with Abraham, Isaac and Jacob. 25He saw the Israelites and knew. . . .

3:1Meanwhile Moses was tending the flock of his father-in-law Jethro, the priest of Midian. Leading the flock across the desert, he came to Horeb, the mountain of God. 2There an angel of the LORD appeared to him in fire flaming out of a bush. As he looked on, he was surprised to see that the bush, though on fire, was not consumed. 3So Moses decided, "I must go over to look at this remarkable sight, and see why the bush is not burned."

4When the LORD saw him coming over to look at it more closely, God called out to him from the bush, "Moses! Moses!" He answered, "Here I am." 5God said, "Come no nearer! Remove the sandals from your feet, for the place where you stand is holy ground. 6I am the God of your father," he continued, "the God of Abraham, the God of Isaac, the God of Jacob." Moses hid his face, for he was afraid to look at God. 7But the LORD said, "I have witnessed the affliction of my people in Egypt and have heard their cry of complaint against their slave drivers, so I know well what they are suffering. 8Therefore I have come down to rescue them from the hands of the Egyptians and lead them out of that land into a good and spacious land, a land flowing with milk and honey, the country of the Canaanites, Hittites, Amorites, Perizzites, Hivites and Jebusites. 9So indeed the cry of the Israelites has reached me, and I have truly noted that the Egyptians are oppressing them. 10Come, now! I will send you to Pharaoh to lead my people, the Israelites, out of Egypt."

11But Moses said to God, "Who am I that I should go to Pharaoh and lead the Israelites out of Egypt?" 12He answered, "I will be with you; and this shall be your proof that it is I who have

> sent you: when you bring my people out of Egypt, you will worship God on this very mountain." [13]"But," said Moses to God, "when I go to the Israelites and say to them, 'The God of your fathers has sent me to you,' if they ask me, 'What is his name?' what am I to tell them?" [14]God replied, "I am who am." Then he added, "This is what you shall tell the Israelites: I AM sent me to you."

Moses fled Egypt for the land of Midian (Exod 2:15). This is not so much a place with specified boundaries as it is a people known for wandering with their flocks in a general region. Moses, who is in flight from Egypt, has become allied by marriage with nomads (Exod 2:15-21) and now wanders the land in order to find pasture and water for his father-in-law's sheep. This makes Moses a double wanderer, twice a pilgrim. In Exodus 2:22 Moses acknowledges his status by naming his firstborn "Gershom," because he associates the name with a Hebrew word for "stranger," which aptly describes his own circumstances: "I am a stranger in a foreign land."

The journey Moses is on might be called a self-imposed exile. He is a wanted criminal in Egypt, at least while the Pharaoh at the time Moses slew the Egyptian was still alive. At this point, Moses is not answering a call; he is avoiding capture. The Hebrew people, however, find no release from their slavery. They cry out in their agony and their cry reaches God. This is the same God of whom the psalmist will later warn all kings and tyrants: "[H]e rescues the poor when they cry out, / the oppressed who have no one to help" (Ps 72:12). God responds to their pleas by calling Moses into service as a prophet and liberator of the people, but Moses is very dubious: "Who am I that I should go to Pharaoh and lead the Israelites out of Egypt" (3:11)?

God calls Moses by speaking through flames from a bush that suffers no harm from the fire. This image is a favorite one of mystics because it seems to vividly illustrate the state of the human soul indwelt by the Spirit of God. How can the Almighty dwell in mortal flesh without destroying us? God remains God and yet the creature not only survives but is transformed in the process of making God visible to the world. God calls Moses, but tells him not to come too near. The presence of God makes the very ground beneath his feet holy, and so Moses is told to remove his sandals. He has, after all, been following sheep in them and they would be caked with dung.

God calls Moses because God has a plan. Moses is to be used as God's prophet to liberate the children of Israel from Egypt. But what "god" is this that has such a plan? Moses wants to know the name of this god (3:13). God has already revealed himself to Moses: "I am the God of your father . . . the God of Abraham, the God of Isaac, the God of Jacob" (3:6). But Moses needs a name, a proper name, not just an association. Why?

People have proper names because each of us is a unique person, a "someone" rather than an "it." We give names to everything we believe we have a special relationship with, including pets and, for some, even plants and automobiles. When God created the world it was said to have been left unfinished, for none of the creatures had names. Naming the things of creation was a task God gave the first human (Gen 2:19). The names he gave to them identified what they were. God actually brought the animals to the human to discover what the human would call them, because whatever the human called them, that's what the creature would be for God!

Moses wants to know God's name because he wants to know who God is. Moses wants to have a relationship with God and he knows that the Hebrew people will also want to know who God is. But naming God is dangerous. Just as Moses cannot come too near God, he cannot expect to get a name for God that puts God at his beck and call. This is another benefit of naming something. When you have someone's name you can use it to call them into your presence. A mother shouts out a child's name and expects not just an answer, but the child's attention. This God has called out "Moses," and Moses, as was proper, responded, "Here I am" (3:4). Moses is not to think he can get the same response from God just because he is given God's name.

And so the name God tells Moses is a mystery. Down through the ages theologians have tried to explain what this name, "I am who am" (often translated, "I am that I am"), means. More recently, biblical scholars have awoken to the probability that God was telling Moses, "Who I am is who I am and you aren't going to get any other answer!"

Due to a sense of deep reverence and a fear of transgressing the command against its misuse, **the sacred name of God**—*Yahweh* (written in ancient Hebrew without vowels as *YHWH* and often translated as "I am")—was omitted from common speech in Judaism and eventually from liturgical practice as well. Instead, when reading Scripture aloud, if the tetragrammaton (Greek for "four letters") *YHWH* was encountered, devout Jews substituted with the term *Adonai* (my Lord). God's further self-identification in Exodus as "the God of Abraham, the God of Isaac, and the God of Jacob" links his present intervention in human history to his covenantal relationship with the patriarchs (see Matt 22:32; Mark 12:26; Luke 20:37).

But God has revealed the relationship Moses is looking for, and he did so even before Moses asked for God's name: "I will be with you; and this shall be your proof that it is I who have sent you: when you bring my people out of Egypt, you will worship God on this very mountain" (3:12). The God who calls Moses, the God who is sending him to Egypt, is the God who will be with him and who will deliver the Hebrew people from slavery and bring them to the mountain where Moses is now standing. It is there that this God will announce the covenant that will bind this people in relationship to their unnameable God for all time. Moses will be leading the people of God on a pilgrimage that will change not only them but all their descendants for all time.

The Song of Moses

Exodus 15:1-18

^{15:1}Then Moses and the Israelites sang this song to the Lord:

²I will sing to the Lord, for he is gloriously
    triumphant;
  horse and chariot he has cast into the sea.
My strength and my courage is the Lord,
    and he has been my savior.
He is my God, I praise him;
    the God of my father, I extol him.
³The Lord is a warrior,
    Lord is his name!
⁴Pharaoh's chariots and army he hurled into
    the sea;
  the elite of his officers were submerged in
    the Red Sea.

⁵The flood waters covered them,
  they sank into the depths like a stone.

⁶Your right hand, O Lord, magnificent in
    power,
  your right hand, O Lord, has shattered
    the enemy.
⁷In your great majesty you overthrew your
    adversaries;
  you loosed your wrath to consume them
    like stubble.
⁸At a breath of your anger the waters piled up,
  the flowing waters stood like a mound,
  the flood waters congealed in the midst of
    the sea.

⁹The enemy boasted, "I will pursue and
    overtake them;

I will divide the spoils and have my fill of
them;
I will draw my sword; my hand shall
despoil them!"
¹⁰When your wind blew, the sea covered them;
like lead they sank in the mighty waters.

¹¹Who is like to you among the gods,
O LORD?
Who is like to you, magnificent in
holiness?
O terrible in renown, worker of wonders,
¹²when you stretched out your right hand,
the earth swallowed them!
¹³In your mercy you led the people you
redeemed;
in your strength you guided them to your
holy dwelling.
¹⁴The nations heard and quaked;
anguish gripped the dwellers in Philistia.
¹⁵Then were the princes of Edom dismayed;
trembling seized the chieftains of Moab;
All the dwellers in Canaan melted away;
¹⁶terror and dread fell upon them.
By the might of your arm they were frozen
like stone,
while your people, O LORD, passed over,
while the people you had made your own
passed over.

¹⁷And you brought them in and planted
them on the mountain of your
inheritance—
the place where you made your seat,
O LORD,
the sanctuary, O LORD, which your hands
established.

¹⁸The LORD shall reign forever and ever.

The Exodus of God's people from Egypt and their journey to a homeland of God's own making is the core story of the Bible. Whether Christian or Jew, whatever we read in the Bible will in some way be related to this foundational story. The Exodus tells us that God's purpose in acting in human history is to re-deem humanity from its slavery. Whether the slavery is a literal one in which human beings are bought and sold as commercial items, or the bondage to sin that afflicts all humanity, it is the biblical account of the Exodus that reveals how God approaches the problem. Our God is a liberator.

The actual account of the Exodus is a much longer story than the verses selected here, but these verses are special because they celebrate the event itself in song. The song is attributed to Moses. It is in the words of this song that a multitude of generations learned and passed on to others the story of their liberation under Moses's leadership. At its heart is the refrain, "Sing to the LORD, for he is gloriously triumphant; / horse and chariot he has cast into the sea" (15:1). This refrain is repeated in 15:21, where it is Moses' sister Miriam who leads all of Israel in giving joyful voice to its words. It is speculated that Miriam's simple refrain came first, and flowered into Moses' song over time.

As a song, these words celebrate God's victory over evil in setting Israel free. We are not just reading about an event in the past. The power and the victory of the Exodus event is encountered in the act of celebrating it. The words summon us to shout, to sing out, to proclaim the reality of the Exodus in the lives of all who will embrace it.

Israel has been set free from its slavery, but not without the hot pursuit of their enslavers (15:9), who would have crushed them under the wheels of their chariots rather than lose their power over them. Freedom has its enemies, but they foolishly fail to reckon with the warrior of freedom, whose name is the Lord (15:3).

As a model story of liberation, the Exodus story also tells us that liberation, from whatever kind of slavery or oppression, sets us on a journey of faith. Free from the threat of Pharaoh and his chariots, the Israelites are on their way to an encounter with God that will bind them in a covenant relationship with God. They have been set free from earthly masters, but their freedom depends on their being bound to a heavenly one. It is not enough to be set free; as free people we must have a firm sense of direction. We must know what our freedom is for and where we are going with it!

That this song helps reveal to Christians their own story of salvation is made clear by its inclusion in the readings for the Easter Vigil Mass, when the elect of God (the catechumens who have been chosen to receive the sacraments of initiation) enter into new life in Christ by passing through the waters of baptism.

While the song is said to be one Moses himself sang, it has obviously been fitted for use by every generation since Moses. In 15:17 the focus on God's saving deed is retrospective: "[Y]ou brought them in and planted them on the mountain of your inheritance." As a song, then, it celebrates the entire journey of God's people, from freedom from slavery to the freedom of responsibility to live the life God has set them free to live. The journey Israel makes between passing through the waters of the sea until their arrival in the Promised Land is an eventful one, however, and deserves our attention in closer detail.

Would that We Had Died in Egypt

Exodus 16:1-3

> 16:1 Having set out from Elim, the whole Israelite community came into the desert of Sin, which is between Elim and Sinai, on the fifteenth day of the second month after their departure from the land of Egypt. 2 Here in the desert the whole Israelite community grumbled against Moses and Aaron. 3 The Israelites said to them, "Would that we had died at the LORD's hand in the land of Egypt, as we sat by our fleshpots and ate our fill of bread! But you had to lead us into this desert to make the whole community die of famine!"

Some people have profound religious experiences that so alter the way they see themselves and their place in the world that all of life is understood as taking place before or after that event. The traditional way of marking the years of history as either "BC" or "AD" is all about seeing time and history itself as a before and after the coming of Jesus Christ. There are, however, billions of people who are not Christians who understandably do not regard history to be solely about the event we Christians see as all important. Likewise, there are many Christians, probably the overwhelming majority, who have not had a religious experience so profound that their whole life seems shaped around it.

Yet even without an earthshaking religious experience, most Christians probably pray for God's guidance in their lives and look for signs, however subtle, that God has led them through the years. What happens when an event occurs, or a situation arises, that makes us wonder, "Where is God in all this?"

As the events surrounding the Exodus are presented to us, it seems so obvious that God intervened in history to save the Hebrew people. A wind divided the waters to let them pass through the sea untouched. When warriors pursued them, the towering sea walls slapped back together and drowned their enemies and swept away their chariots. The Lord then led the people away from Egypt, guiding them all the while by a column of cloud by day and a column of fire by night (Exod 13:21). Could anyone doubt that the hand of God was upon them to deliver them from all evil?

It seems they all doubted it. Everyone except Moses, and perhaps a few others, grumbled, "Would that we had died at the LORD's hand in the land of Egypt, as we sat by our fleshpots and ate our fill of bread! But you had to lead us into this desert to make the whole community die of famine!" (Exod 16:3).

We can assume that before the verbal grumbling started, the grumbling of their stomachs was sending up alarms. They were in a desert and there was no food. Who was going to feed them? Where would food possibly come from?

Food and Drink

Exodus 16:4-15

Doubt and Grumbling

Exodus 17:1-7

16:4Then the LORD said to Moses, "I will now rain down bread from heaven for you. Each day the people are to go out and gather their daily portion; thus will I test them, to see whether they follow my instructions or not. 5On the sixth day, however, when they prepare what they bring in, let it be twice as much as they gather on the other days." 6So Moses and Aaron told all the Israelites, "At evening you will know that it was the LORD who brought you out of the land of Egypt; 7and in the morning you will see the glory of the LORD, as he heeds your grumbling against him. But what are we that you should grumble against us? 8When the LORD gives you flesh to eat in the evening," continued Moses, "and in the morning your fill of bread, as he heeds the grumbling you utter against him, what then are we? Your grumbling is not against us, but against the LORD."

9Then Moses said to Aaron, "Tell the whole Israelite community: Present yourselves before the LORD, for he has heard your grumbling." 10When Aaron announced this to the whole Israelite community, they turned toward the desert, and lo, the glory of the LORD appeared in the cloud! 11The LORD spoke to Moses and said, 12"I have heard the grumbling of the Israelites. Tell them: In the evening twilight you shall eat flesh, and in the morning you shall have your fill of bread, so that you may know that I, the LORD, am your God."

13In the evening quail came up and covered the camp. In the morning a dew lay all about the camp, 14and when the dew evaporated, there on the surface of the desert were fine flakes like hoarfrost on the ground. 15On seeing it, the Israelites asked one another, "What is this?" for they did not know what it was. But Moses told them, "This is the bread which the LORD has given you to eat."

17:1From the desert of Sin the whole Israelite community journeyed by stages, as the LORD directed, and encamped at Rephidim.

Here there was no water for the people to drink. 2They quarreled, therefore, with Moses and said, "Give us water to drink." Moses replied, "Why do you quarrel with me? Why do you put the LORD to a test?" 3Here, then, in their thirst for water, the people grumbled against Moses, saying, "Why did you ever make us leave Egypt? Was it just to have us die here of thirst with our children and our livestock?" 4So Moses cried out to the LORD, "What shall I do with this people? A little more and they will stone me!" 5The LORD answered Moses, "Go over there in front of the people, along with some of the elders of Israel, holding in your hand, as you go, the staff with which you struck the river. 6I will be standing there in front of you on the rock in Horeb. Strike the rock, and the water will flow from it for the people to drink." This Moses did, in the presence of the elders of Israel. 7The place was called Massah and Meribah, because the Israelites quarreled there and tested the LORD, saying, "Is the LORD in our midst or not?"

God miraculously feeds the people on their journey. What began with signs and wonders continues with signs and wonders, but the people seem almost oblivious. Whatever they need, their needs are met, but in each discovery of a new need there is a renewed doubt that God is taking care of them. Once again, this poses the question for us: how do we respond when life situations and events occur that give us ample reason to wonder, "Where is God?"

After experiencing numerous miracles it seems a shocking thing to doubt God, but what supports our faith when the need for a miracle has come and gone and left us wanting? It is then that faith becomes its own miracle. Eating and drinking are necessary to sustain life and these things God pours out generously to the children of Israel in the dry, barren wilderness. But what God is waiting for them to discover is that they have not gone into the wilderness in order to be fed; rather, they have gone there to find God. God can only be found with faith. The gift of faith, then, is the miracle to ask for in life, for it can sustain purpose and meaning in life even after all else is taken away.

Faithfulness to God is the ultimate purpose behind God's allowing the people to wander in the wilderness for forty years, day by day depending on God for everything. This is made clear in the words of the prophet Moses to the people at the end of their wilderness journey, just before they are to enter the Promised Land (Deut 8:3a-5):

> He therefore let you be afflicted with hunger, and then fed you with manna, a food unknown to you and your fathers, in order to show you that not by bread alone does man live, but by every word that comes forth from the mouth of the LORD. The clothing did not fall from you in tatters, nor did your feet swell these forty years. So you must realize that the LORD, your God, disciplines you even as a man disciplines his son.

Why are the people ready now, after forty years, to enter the Promised Land? What has changed for them? They have something from God that is better than bread, sturdier than well-shod shoes. They are equipped for their journey with the "word that comes forth from the mouth of the LORD." God spoke this word to them through Moses. Through Moses, God delivered to them the ten "words" (commandments) with the power to guide them safely through the moral dilemmas of life while providing the foundation for a just society.

Several attempts have been made to identify a natural source for the **manna** that fed the Israelites in the desert, including certain forms of fructifying lichen, a honey-like residue secreted by the tamarisk bush, or excretions by insects that feed on the tamarisk's leaves. Whatever the source, it is clear that the sacred author understands the appearance of this food as a miraculous event. Many of the Church Fathers—St. Irenaeus, St. Ambrose, and St. Augustine among them—saw in the manna a sign or precursor of the Eucharist (see John 6:31-59).

Ten Commandments

Deuteronomy 5:6-21

5:6"I, the LORD, am your God, who brought you out of the land of Egypt, that place of slavery. 7You shall not have other gods besides me. 8You shall not carve idols for yourselves in the shape of anything in the sky above or on the earth below or in the waters beneath the earth; 9you shall not bow down before them or worship them. For I, the LORD, your God, am a jealous God, inflicting punishments for their fathers' wickedness on the children of those who hate me, down to the third and fourth generation 10but bestowing mercy, down to the thousandth generation, on the children of those who love me and keep my commandments.

11"You shall not take the name of the LORD, your God, in vain. For the LORD will not leave unpunished him who takes his name in vain.

12"Take care to keep holy the sabbath day as the LORD, your God, commanded you. 13Six days you may labor and do all your work; 14but the seventh day is the sabbath of the LORD, your God. No work may be done then, whether by you, or your son or daughter, or your male or female slave,

continue

or your ox or ass or any of your beasts, or the alien who lives with you. Your male and female slave should rest as you do. [15]For remember that you too were once slaves in Egypt, and the LORD, your God, brought you from there with his strong hand and outstretched arm. That is why the LORD, your God, has commanded you to observe the sabbath day.

[16]"Honor your father and your mother, as the LORD, your God, has commanded you, that you may have a long life and prosperity in the land which the LORD, your God, is giving you.

[17]"You shall not kill.

[18]"You shall not commit adultery.

[19]"You shall not steal.

[20]"You shall not bear dishonest witness against your neighbor.

[21]"You shall not covet your neighbor's wife.

"You shall not desire your neighbor's house or field, nor his male or female slave, nor his ox or ass, nor anything that belongs to him."

Within Catholic tradition there is the understanding that the morality found in the Ten Commandments is also enshrined in our consciences and recognizable by human reason. This means even those individuals and cultures who have never heard of God's special revelation to Moses and the children of Israel have the moral resources to guide them along a very similar path as what is directed in the Ten Commandments. It is said that even the obligation to set aside a day for rest and contemplation of our highest good (God) might be arrived at simply through rational reflection.

There is, however, a very special aspect to the revelation of the Ten Commandments that goes beyond morality as reason alone might teach us. The very first few words of the Ten Commandments give us something we can't claim to know by our own thought processes, no matter how intelligent we are: "I, the LORD, am *your* God" (emphasis added).

The first commandment begins with a declaration of a special relationship with God that God makes possible in giving Israel these commandments. Here, God declares that these moral imperatives are both a gift and an obligation that are a response to a God who loves us personally. No matter how reasonable they are, keeping these commandments has the added spiritual quality of witnessing to our covenanted relationship with the Creator. That God wants to be a part of our lives makes the Ten Commandments part of a special covenant rather than just another time-honored code of ethics.

"When someone asks him, 'Which commandment in the Law is the greatest?' Jesus replies: 'You shall love the Lord your God with all your heart, and with all your soul, and with all your mind. This is the greatest and first commandment. And a second is like it: You shall love your neighbor as yourself. On these two commandments hang all the Law and the prophets' (Matt 22:37-40; cf. Deut 6:5; Lev 19:18). The Decalogue must be interpreted in light of this twofold yet **single commandment of love**, the fullness of the Law" (*Catechism of the Catholic Church* 2055, emphasis added).

Not everywhere we go in life is in the footsteps of others. If the path was well worn from the successful journeys of many pilgrims, we would know which way to turn. Morality, especially one grounded in the Ten Commandments, is meant to be an inner guide, the voice of a well-informed conscience, that gives us direction even when our path in life is otherwise ill-defined. The Ten Commandments assure us not only that we can know right from wrong but that God is our companion in the journey.

Moses on Mount Nebo

Deuteronomy 32:49-51

> 32:49"Go up on Mount Nebo, here in the Abarim Mountains [it is in the land of Moab facing Jericho], and view the land of Canaan, which I am giving to the Israelites as their possession. 50Then you shall die on the mountain you have climbed, and shall be taken to your people, just as your brother Aaron died on Mount Hor and there was taken to his people; 51because both of you broke faith with me among the Israelites at the waters of Meribath-kadesh in the desert of Zin by failing to manifest my sanctity among the Israelites."

Forty years have passed since Israel left Egypt. Moses is going to die before the people complete their pilgrimage. This is one of the enduring mysteries of Scripture. Moses, the great prophet through whom God delivered the Ten Commandments to Israel, the liberator who, through his dependence on God, led Israel away from slavery in Egypt, dies without the opportunity to enter the land God promised to the people he led. Jesus, in the Sermon on the Mount, promises that the meek shall inherit the land (Matt 5:5), and yet Moses, whom Numbers calls the meekest man on the face of the earth (Num 12:3), dies after only being able to look upon the Promised Land from a distant mountain.

Moses was not perfect. He complained that the burden of God's people was too great for him (Exod 17:4). At Meribath-kadesh, when he was told to strike the rock that would pour out water for the people in their thirst, he was angry and struck the rock twice. This, it seems, is how Moses failed to manifest God's sanctity among the Israelites. At least we are not given anything else to account for Moses' punishment. But Moses was also willing to die for the people in pleading for God's mercy on them (32:31-32).

In later assessment, however, the New Testament letter to the Hebrews asserts that,

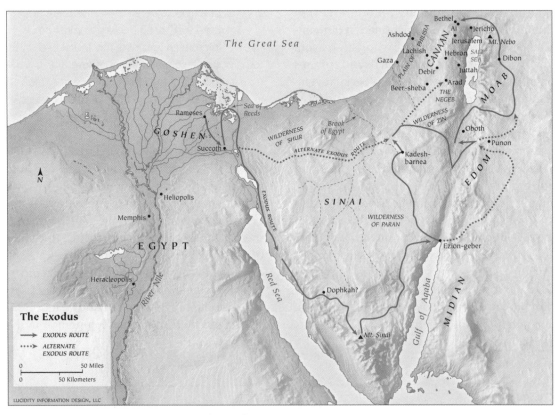

The Great Sea

The Exodus

→ EXODUS ROUTE

••••▶ ALTERNATE EXODUS ROUTE

0   50 Miles

0   50 Kilometers

LUCIDITY INFORMATION DESIGN, LLC

"Moses was 'faithful in all his house'" (Heb 3:5). Whatever his failures, Moses is remembered in Scripture as the key figure in Old Testament revelation.

Moses had given his life to leading his people into the land of God's promise. Imagine what it must have meant to Moses to learn that he would die without entering it himself! It must have been the bitterest disappointment, losing his highest ambition. And yet, throughout Moses' pilgrimage of faith, including the experience of the Exodus and the forty years of wandering in the wilderness, his purpose in life had been first and foremost to carry out the will of God. Whether his achievements fell short of his ambition in life or not, his death was marked out for him as an opportunity to accomplish God's will. He is told beforehand where he will die and he makes that one last journey under God's direction.

God's Words to Joshua

Joshua 1:1-11

> 1:1After Moses, the servant of the LORD, had died, the LORD said to Moses' aide Joshua, son of Nun: 2"My servant Moses is dead. So prepare to cross the Jordan here, with all the people, into the land I will give the Israelites. 3As I promised Moses, I will deliver to you every place where you set foot. 4Your domain is to be all the land of the Hittites, from the desert and from Lebanon east to the great river Euphrates and west to the Great Sea. 5No one can withstand you while you live. I will be with you as I was with Moses: I will not leave you nor forsake you. 6Be firm and steadfast, so that you may give this people possession of the land which I swore to their fathers I would give them. 7Above all, be firm and steadfast, taking care to observe the entire law which my servant Moses enjoined on you. Do not swerve from it either to the right or to the left, that you may succeed wherever you go. 8Keep this book of the law

> on your lips. Recite it by day and by night, that you may observe carefully all that is written in it; then you will successfully attain your goal. 9I command you: be firm and steadfast! Do not fear nor be dismayed, for the LORD, your God, is with you wherever you go."
>
> 10So Joshua commanded the officers of the people: 11"Go through the camp and instruct the people, 'Prepare your provisions, for three days from now you shall cross the Jordan here, to march in and take possession of the land which the LORD, your God, is giving you.'"

Joshua is now God's chosen one to lead Israel into the Promised Land. Sooner or later a transition like this happens to most of us in life. Someone we have depended on for leadership, inspiration, or guidance moves away, retires, or dies. And then we realize we are the new leader. We are the one chosen to guide, inspire, and perhaps even command. God's word to Joshua might well be needed at such a transition in life: "I will be with you as I was with Moses: I will not leave you nor forsake you. Be firm and steadfast" (1:5b-6a).

Entering the Promised Land

Joshua 3:14-17

> 3:14The people struck their tents to cross the Jordan, with the priests carrying the ark of the covenant ahead of them. 15No sooner had these priestly bearers of the ark waded into the waters at the edge of the Jordan, which overflows all its banks during the entire season of the harvest, 16than the waters flowing from upstream halted, backing up in a solid mass for a very great distance indeed, from Adam, a city in the direction of Zarethan; while those flowing downstream toward the Salt Sea of the Arabah disappeared entirely. Thus the people
> *continue*

43

crossed over opposite Jericho. [17]While all Israel crossed over on dry ground, the priests carrying the ark of the covenant of the LORD remained motionless on dry ground in the bed of the Jordan until the whole nation had completed the passage.

The book of Joshua describes Israel's entry into the Promised Land as something that is done not only miraculously but also with military precision and purpose. They are not just going into the land; they are going into a land with many armed inhabitants with the purpose of taking possession of it away from them. If you were a Canaanite, you would probably regard this as an invasion. Much in theology, Scripture, and the assumptions made in the context of Judeo-Christian heritage have taught many of us to see this land as God's gift to the children of Israel. Through the long course of postbiblical history, however, the land known as both Palestine and Israel has become the rightful home of many people, and the perspectives of particular theologies that would limit the claims to the land to only one particular people run the risk of creating victims of untold violence for generations to come.

The land Joshua led the people into was called Canaan. While the books of Joshua and Judges frequently describe their entry as a violent conquest, there are also passages within them that suggest a more peaceful growth of their culture and religion within the land that would eventually be called Israel (e.g., Josh 9:3-15; 13:13). Whether by conquest, cultural proliferation, or a combination of both, the many tribes of Israel would eventually become a single nation, with its capital Jerusalem within the section named for Judah, the tribe of Israel from which all Jews today have garnered their identity.

As we shall see, their possession of the land proves to be quite tenuous. The northern tribes of Israel will be completely dispossessed of it in 721 BC by an imponderable force of Assyrians led by Shalmaneser and Sargon II (2 Kgs 17:6). In 587 BC, the rest of the children of Israel, the inhabitants of Jerusalem and Judah, were driven from the Promised Land into Babylon (modern day Iraq) by Nebuchadnezzar (2 Kgs 25:1-12).

EXPLORING LESSON TWO

1. What examples of irony (an outcome contrary to what is expected) do you find in the infancy narrative of Moses (Exod 1:12b–2:10)?

_____

_____

_____

_____

2. Like many other pivotal figures in the Bible (e.g., Abraham, Samson, Saul, David, Peter), Moses is a flawed character. He is prone to anger and violence (Exod 2:11-12) and is reluctant to take on the mission God has prepared for him (Exod 3:11). Why do you think God persists in choosing Moses as the instrument by which he will liberate the Israelites?

_____

_____

_____

_____

3. While enduring self-imposed exile in Midian, Moses feels the burden of being a resident alien in a foreign land (Exod 2:22). To what extent are we as Christians also strangers in a foreign land? (See 2 Cor 5:1-9; Eph 2:19-20.)

_____

_____

_____

_____

4. a) Why is it so important for Moses to know God's name (Exod 3:13)?

_____

_____

_____

_____

b) In what way does the name of God, though revealed, remain mysterious?

_____

_____

_____

_____

5. What message does the Exodus proclaim concerning God's intervention in human history?

_____

_____

_____

_____

_____

6. The story of Exodus tells of the Israelites' liberation from earthly bondage in Egypt, but it also relates how they came to serve a new, heavenly master through the covenant of Sinai. In the New Testament, Paul explores this paradox further, explaining that while we have been freed from slavery to sin, we have in turn become "slaves to righteousness" (Rom 6:16-22). What does it mean for Christians to find their freedom in being "slaves of God" (1 Pet 2:16)? How might we understand "slavery" in this context?

_____

_____

_____

_____

_____

7. Despite witnessing many miracles associated with their deliverance from Egypt, the Israelites remain convinced that they will not have enough food to sustain them on their journey though the desert (Exod 16:3). What lessons about faith can we draw from God's response to the Israelites' concerns?

_____

_____

_____

_____

8. Beyond the Ten Commandments (Deut 5:6-21) and the love commands (Matt 22:37-40; John 13:34), what are some important rules of life that you have personally embraced as "inner guides"? Were these "revealed" to you, or did they emerge from your own conscience?

_____

_____

_____

_____

_____

9. a) Why was Moses not permitted to enter the Promised Land (Deut 32:49-51)?

_____

_____

_____

_____

b) What can we learn from Moses' acceptance of this disappointment?

_____

_____

_____

_____

10. a) After Moses' death, God chooses Joshua to lead the Israelites into the Promised Land. What words of encouragement does God give Joshua as he prepares to assume leadership (Josh 1:1-9)?

_____

_____

_____

_____

b) Have you ever had to step in and assume a leadership role left vacant by someone else? What support did you receive from others that proved most helpful as you began your service? What resistance or obstacles did you have to overcome?

_____

_____

_____

_____

What's our liberation from ① ourselves, our own ego,
② doing things alone — need to be something/someone
we have a community to rely on,
to work with

think of Exodus as a mold of our lives.

CLOSING PRAYER

Prayer

Moses agreed to live with him, and the man gave him his daughter Zipporah in marriage. She bore him a son, whom he named Gershom; for he said, "I am a stranger in a foreign land." (Exod 2:21-22)

Loving God, as we strive to heed your call and follow the path of discipleship, may we not forget those among us who struggle to find their way. We pray for all those who feel alienated, lost, or abandoned; for the poor, the homeless, and the dispossessed; for migrants, refugees, and the victims of war or abuse; for those who are sick or in pain; for those who struggle with addiction. May we demonstrate our love for you by the compassion that we show to all of our fellow pilgrims. Today we especially pray for . . .

LESSON THREE

Exile and Return

Begin your personal study and group discussion with a simple and sincere prayer such as:

Prayer

God, you are the source and goal of all life. Strengthen, support, and guide us on our earthly pilgrimage so that, nourished by your word and inspired by your Son's example, we may persevere in faith until we find ourselves home at last in your heavenly kingdom.

Read pages 50–63, Lesson Three

Respond to the questions on pages 64–66, Exploring Lesson Three.

The Closing Prayer on page 66 is for your personal use and may be used at the end of group discussion.

Lesson Three

EXILE AND RETURN

Pilgrimage to the Temple

Psalm 122

> [122:1] I rejoiced when they said to me,
> "Let us go to the house of the LORD."
> [2] And now our feet are standing
> within your gates, Jerusalem.
> [3] Jerusalem, built as a city,
> walled round about.
> [4] Here the tribes have come,
> the tribes of the LORD,
> As it was decreed for Israel,
> to give thanks to the name of the LORD.
> [5] Here are the thrones of justice,
> the thrones of the house of David.
>
> [6] For the peace of Jerusalem pray:
> "May those who love you prosper!"
> [7] May peace be within your ramparts,
> prosperity within your towers."
> [8] For family and friends I say,
> "May peace be yours."
> [9] For the house of the LORD, our God, I pray,
> "May blessings be yours."

The first temple dedicated to the exclusive worship of Israel's God was built by King Solomon between 966–59 BC. In its time it would have been not just impressive but awe-inspiring in its majesty. By today's standards it was not such a large building. Its physical dimensions, according to McKenzie's *Dictionary of the Bible*, are said to have been only ninety feet long by thirty feet wide by forty-five feet high.

There is no real claim in Scripture that the temple could actually house God in some finite fashion. Solomon himself acknowledges in 1 Kings 8:27 that "The heavens and the highest heavens cannot contain you, how much less this temple which I have built!" In Psalm 132:7 the temple is referred to as God's footstool. Nevertheless, to one of the Lord's faithful worshipers, who would have traveled to the temple from some distance in order to pray and have sacri-

fices offered, the temple was a place in which God did dwell in a very special way. The temple was a glorious sign that God lived in the midst of Israel's people. God had directed no other people on earth to build such a dwelling.

Psalm 122 is called a song of ascent. This means that it was a song sung by pilgrims as they climbed the hillsides toward Jerusalem and finally up to the temple mount itself. Even without musical notation, these psalms resound with the joy of arriving at the goal of a pilgrimage.

A pilgrimage is traditionally understood as a journey made to a specific destination solely for a religious purpose. While the popularity of making a pilgrimage has declined in recent centuries among Christians, during the Middle Ages churches throughout Europe and especially sites associated with Christ in the Holy Land drew endless streams of devout pilgrims, many of whom had to beg for food and shelter on their journeys. Because a pilgrimage was most often undertaken on foot and required anything from days to weeks or even months to complete, a pilgrimage demanded complete dedication. All of life's activities would become reoriented toward reaching the destination and fulfilling the religious obligation associated with the destination.

The destination that marks the physical end of a journey may be described as the goal of a pilgrimage, but not its purpose. The purpose of a pilgrimage is to arrive at a more profound relationship with God. By dedicating all of one's physical activity to completing the journey, all the while attuning one's heart and mind to the task, the pilgrim experiences a transformation of self. This is the gladness that fills the hearts of the pilgrims in Psalm 122. The temple has come in sight, the presence of the God who has called them to this special place and to a special act of worship is very near to them; the joy that fills the psalm leaves no room to doubt it.

In Psalm 122 we hear that Jerusalem is doubly special, doubly holy. Not only is it the site of the temple, where "it was decreed for Israel, / to give thanks to the name of the LORD," (v. 4b), it is also the site of the "thrones of justice, / the thrones of the house of David" (v. 5). It is in Jerusalem that God's special presence in Israel's midst can be tangibly experienced through the sign of the temple, and it is from Jerusalem that God's just governance of Israel is dispensed through the royal dynasty of God's own choosing. These are the kings descended from David, who rule by God's will, according to the promise given to David by God through Nathan the prophet, as found in 2 Samuel 7:16. "Your house and your kingdom shall endure forever before me; your throne shall stand firm forever."

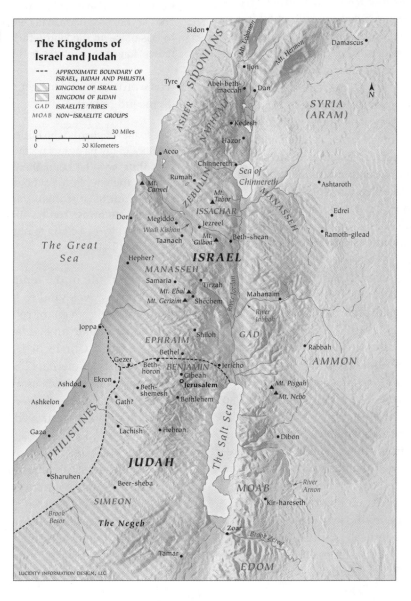

The Kingdoms of Israel and Judah

--- APPROXIMATE BOUNDARY OF ISRAEL, JUDAH AND PHILISTIA
KINGDOM OF ISRAEL
KINGDOM OF JUDAH
GAD ISRAELITE TRIBES
MOAB NON-ISRAELITE GROUPS

0   30 Miles
0   30 Kilometers

Sidon
Damascus
Mt. Lebanon
Ijon
Mt. Hermon
Tyre
SIDONIANS
Abel-beth-maccah
Dan
ASHER
NAPHTALI
SYRIA (ARAM)
Kedesh
Hazor
Acco
Chinnereth
ZEBULUN
Sea of Chinnereth
Ashtaroth
Rumah
Mt. Carmel
Mt. Tabor
MANASSEH
Dor
Megiddo
ISSACHAR
Jezreel
Edrei
Wadi Kishon
Mt. Gilboa
Beth-shean
Ramoth-gilead
Taanach
The Great Sea
Hepher?
MANASSEH
ISRAEL
Samaria
Tirzah
Mahanaim
Mt. Ebal
Mt. Gerizim
Shechem
River Jabbok
Joppa
River Jordan
EPHRAIM
Shiloh
GAD
Bethel
Rabbah
Gezer
Beth-horon
BENJAMIN
Jericho
AMMON
Gibeah
Ashdod
Ekron
Jerusalem
Mt. Pisgah
Beth-shemesh
Mt. Nebo
Ashkelon
Gath?
Bethlehem
PHILISTINES
Lachish
Hebron
The Salt Sea
Gaza
Dibon
JUDAH
Sharuhen
Beer-sheba
MOAB
River Arnon
SIMEON
Kir-hareseth
Brook Besor
The Negeb
Zoar
Brook Zered
Tamar
EDOM

LUCIDITY INFORMATION DESIGN, LLC

This promise to David was short-lived outside of the southern territories of Judah and Benjamin. When David's grandson Rehoboam succeeded his father Solomon as king (922 BC), he fancied himself capable of bullying the ten northern tribes into paying heavy taxes and working under forced-labor conditions in payment for the privilege of submitting to his rule. After meeting with the northern tribal leaders who sought relief from Solomon's onerous practices, Rehoboam responded by telling them, "My father put on you a heavy yoke, but I will make it heavier. My father beat you with whips, but I will beat you with scorpions" (1 Kgs 12:14).

Civil war erupted, and the northern tribes never again experienced the rule of a king in David's lineage. Both kingdoms claimed to be "Israel," but for the sake of clarity, the southern kingdom came to be most commonly referred to as Judah. The kingdoms remained separate nations for just over two hundred years. Then, in 721 BC, the Assyrians utterly destroyed the northern kingdom of Israel, scattering most of its people throughout its empire and repopulating the land with other conquered peoples.

Shrines of sacrifice and worship were established in the north, but the temple in Jerusalem was adamantly claimed by its priests as the only legitimate place to worship the God who had revealed himself to Moses as YHWH. In the two books of Kings, every northern king, from Jeroboam on, is condemned for allowing sacrificial worship to take place outside the temple in Jerusalem (see 1 Kgs 13:33-34; 2 Kgs 17:20-21).

Before and after the division of the kingdoms, for the loyal pilgrims traveling to Jerusalem, there was no place on earth like its temple, no place else where they could so surely find themselves in the presence of the living God. There they rejoiced, sang praises, and had sacrifices offered to the one who created them, blessed them, and through whom they hoped to be governed in peace and prosperity by the Lord's anointed king (vv. 6-8).

This was the idyllic experience of the ancient pilgrim to Jerusalem. Unfortunately, the religious turmoil of the times often pitted reality against pious expectations. Because of the abject failures of priests and kings alike to live up to their responsibilities, both the temple and the royal house came under the severe criticism of more than one prophet.

Jeremiah warned those who believed that the presence of the temple guaranteed God's blessing and presence not to deceive themselves:

> Put not your trust in the deceitful words: "This is the temple of the LORD! The temple of the LORD! The temple of the LORD!" Only if you thoroughly reform your ways and your deeds; if each of you deals justly with his neighbor; if you no longer oppress the resident alien, the orphan, and the widow; if you no longer shed innocent blood in this place, or follow strange gods to your own harm, will I remain with you in this place, in the land which I gave your fathers long ago and forever. (Jer 7:4-7)

His words to the rulers were also a warning of divine judgment:

> Woe to the shepherds who mislead and scatter the flock of my pasture, says the LORD. Therefore, thus says the LORD, the God of Israel, against the shepherds who shepherd my people: You have scattered my sheep and driven them away. You have not cared for them, but I will take care to punish your evil deeds. (Jer 23:1-2)

Jerusalem, site of the temple and seat of royal authority, was vital to Judah's understanding of their covenant relationship with God. God had made an everlasting covenant with them (see 1 Chr 16:14-18), establishing David's dynasty as eternal (2 Sam 23:1-5) and the worship in the temple as everlasting (Lev 24:8). How could those things be true if Jerusalem itself could be destroyed?

The three festivals for which all male Israelites were originally required to "appear before the LORD" (Deut 16:16) were the feast of Unleavened Bread (closely associated with Passover), the feast of Weeks, and the feast of Booths. In Deuteronomy and Exodus (Exod 23:14-

15, 17; 34:22-23) the destination of these annual pilgrimages is unspecified: the place of sacrifice is only identified as "the place which he [the LORD] chooses." With David's establishment of Jerusalem as the capital of the united kingdom of Israel and the subsequent construction of the first temple there by Solomon, **Jerusalem assumed a primacy** over all other shrines and sanctuaries and became the focus of Jewish worship and sacrifice.

The Fall of Jerusalem

2 Kings 25:1-11

25:1In the tenth month of the ninth year of Zedekiah's reign, on the tenth day of the month, Nebuchadnezzar, king of Babylon, and his whole army advanced against Jerusalem, encamped around it, and built siege walls on every side. 2The siege of the city continued until the eleventh year of Zedekiah. 3On the ninth day of the fourth month, when famine had gripped the city, and the people had no more bread, 4the city walls were breached. Then the king and all the soldiers left the city by night through the gate between the two walls which was near the king's garden. Since the Chaldeans had the city surrounded, they went in the direction of the Arabah. 5But the Chaldean army pursued the king and overtook him in the desert near Jericho, abandoned by his whole army.

6The king was therefore arrested and brought to Riblah to the king of Babylon, who pronounced sentence on him. 7He had Zedekiah's sons slain before his eyes. Then he blinded Zedekiah, bound him with fetters, and had him brought to Babylon.

8On the seventh day of the fifth month (this was in the nineteenth year of Nebuchadnezzar, king of Babylon), Nebuzaradan, captain of the bodyguard, came to Jerusalem as the representative of the king of Babylon. 9He burned the house of the LORD, the palace of the king, and all the houses of Jerusalem; every large building was destroyed by fire. 10Then the Chaldean troops who were with the captain of the guard tore down the walls that surrounded Jerusalem.

11Then Nebuzaradan, captain of the guard, led into exile the last of the people remaining in the city, and those who had deserted to the king of Babylon, and the last of the artisans.

King Nebuchadnezzar of Babylon destroyed Jerusalem and forced the people into exile in 587 BC. Well over a hundred years before that, around 701 BC, the kingdom of Judah had become a vassal state of the Assyrian Empire. In 721 BC Assyria destroyed the much larger and wealthier kingdom of Israel, which comprised ten of the twelve tribes of the Hebrew people. After the Assyrian Empire was conquered by Babylon, Jerusalem became a small, easily snatched prize of war to the Babylonians as well.

While the biblical record is adamant that both Israel and Judah suffered horrendous fates because of their unfaithfulness, historians note that the land on which these two kingdoms were established provided the most convenient route for the mighty warring powers that lay both to the north and to the south. Only when these far superior powers were at their weakest were Israel or Judah ever able to enjoy security within their borders.

Because the city was miraculously protected from Sennacherib and the invading Assyrian army (2 Kgs 19:35-36), the belief grew that Jerusalem was invulnerable. Jerusalem, City of David and City of God, could not be shaken because God was in its midst (Ps 46:6). Kings would always be put to flight because God had established the city to last forever (Ps 48:5-9). This conviction of invulnerability led to abuses, however. God's people assumed that, no matter how they lived, they would be safe in Jerusalem. Jeremiah warns them that simply trusting in the temple of the Lord is not enough; they must live according to the covenant (Jer 7:1-15; cf. Mic 3:12). The **destruction of the temple** by Nebuchadnezzar in 587 BC forced a radical rethinking of the meaning of God's presence among the people.

To whatever extent we regard the exile of the Jews from their homeland in 587 BC as a theological event, it was also a heart-wrenching event of human tragedy whose like gets repeated over and over again throughout human history. Whether the people are Jews or Palestinians, Armenians or Somalis, American Indians or French Canadians, peoples ancient or modern, warfare often causes entire populations to be "vomited out" (see Lev 20:22) of their homes and homelands and forced to march at the end of a spear, a gun, or simply from fear into a strange land with a strange climate and often with a strange language. This too is a pilgrimage, one that might require the greatest faith of all as it works or wracks its transforming effects upon the human soul.

The Jewish people who survived the Babylonian onslaught did not necessarily consider themselves the lucky ones. The book of Lamentations records the survivors' deep sorrow for their city, their civilization, and every aspect of their shattered lives as they are driven from their burnt-out dwellings and prodded forcefully into exile.

Exile

Lamentations 1:1-5

> ¹:¹How lonely she is now,
>   the once crowded city!
> Widowed is she
>   who was mistress over nations;
> The princess among the provinces
>   has been made a toiling slave.

> ²Bitterly she weeps at night,
>   tears upon her cheeks,
> With not one to console her
>   of all her dear ones;
> Her friends have all betrayed her
>   and become her enemies.

> ³Judah has fled into exile
>   from oppression and cruel slavery;
> Yet where she lives among the nations
>   she finds no place to rest:
> All her persecutors come upon her
>   where she is narrowly confined.

> ⁴The roads to Zion mourn
>   for lack of pilgrims going to her feasts;
> All her gateways are deserted,
>   her priests groan,
> Her virgins sigh;
>   she is in bitter grief.

> ⁵Her foes are uppermost,
>   her enemies are at ease;
> The Lᴏʀᴅ has punished her
>   for her many sins.
> Her little ones have gone away,
>   captive before the foe.

The inspired poet behind Lamentations is a witness to the tragedy of impending exile following Jerusalem's destruction. The city's suffering is his own. Without any attempt to hide from the pain, his loss, shared thousands of times over by fellow refugees, is taken fully to heart and expressed with exquisite care.

Using a powerful poetic device that is quite common in Scripture, Lamentations opens by depicting the devastated city of Jerusalem as a person. Filled with the emotions of a once proud mother—a princess—she has endured the loss of everything and everyone dear to her. She is a lonely widow, cast into slavery. She weeps bitterly and has no one to console her. She has been betrayed by those in whom she placed her trust. It is as if a beautiful princess suddenly found herself chased down a dark, dead-end alley by rapacious, cutthroat attackers.

By verse four, the image of Jerusalem returns to that of a city, a beloved city that once knew the joy of expectant worshipers flocking to the roads leading to the temple. But the roads themselves are personified. They mourn for the lack of pilgrims.

Hope in the Lord

Lamentations 3:18-24

> ³:¹⁸I tell myself my future is lost,
>   all that I hoped for from the LORD.
>
> ¹⁹The thought of my homeless poverty
>   is wormwood and gall;
> ²⁰Remembering it over and over
>   leaves my soul downcast within me.
> ²¹But I will call this to mind,
>   as my reason to have hope:
>
> ²²The favors of the LORD are not exhausted,
>   his mercies are not spent;
> ²³They are renewed each morning,
>   so great is his faithfulness.
> ²⁴My portion is the LORD, says my soul;
>   therefore will I hope in him.

In the midst of the greatest tragedy possible for the people of God at this time, with their temple destroyed and all the heirs to David's throne either executed or prisoners of Nebuchadnezzar, this biblical lament turns to confident trust in God. In 3:22 we read that a time will come when God will again bless the people of Judah. And then, in the next verse, this prayer of trust and hope turns even more surprising. God's favors are not just held in store for some future date; they are to be given to the people now, even while they experience the depths of their tragic circumstances: "They are renewed each morning, / so great is his faithfulness."

What are these mercies that God renews every morning? Will the exile end immediately? Are the prisoners marching to Babylon to be freed and told to return home? It would appear that the greatest mercy the exiles are to receive at this time is not the end of their exile, but simply the surprising confidence that arises in the human heart from knowing that their God is with them on the journey, no matter how traumatic a journey it may be.

While their exile remains something extremely bitter, even their woeful complaints that cry out to God in their misery are embedded with a stubborn hope. Psalm 137 captures the bitterness for all time.

Remembering Zion with Tears

Psalm 137:1-6

> ¹³⁷:¹By the rivers of Babylon
>   we sat mourning and weeping
>   when we remembered Zion.
> ²On the poplars of that land
>   we hung up our harps.
> ³There our captors asked us
>   for the words of a song;
> Our tormentors, for a joyful song:
>   "Sing for us a song of Zion!"
> ⁴But how could we sing a song of the LORD
>   in a foreign land?
>
> ⁵If I forget you, Jerusalem,
>   may my right hand wither.
> ⁶May my tongue stick to my palate
>   if I do not remember you,
> If I do not exalt Jerusalem
>   beyond all my delights.

Their bitterness is so great that the Jewish exiles refuse to sing any of their praises of God in the presence of their captors, but their refusal is itself a prayer. It is preserved as a psalm to be prayed over and over by succeeding generations. Today, Psalm 137 has been adapted for use in a modern play about Jesus (*Godspell*) and by others for use in Christian worship.

What time or people or natural disasters have taken away cannot alienate us from our memories of God's faithfulness.

The exiles will not sing before their captors, but neither will they forget their desire to worship God in Jerusalem. Fifty years will pass before the good news is announced. An end to exile, the temple is to be rebuilt!

Return to Jerusalem

Ezra 1:1-6

1:1In the first year of Cyrus, king of Persia, in order to fulfill the word of the LORD spoken by Jeremiah, the LORD inspired King Cyrus of Persia to issue this proclamation throughout his kingdom, both by word of mouth and in writing: 2"Thus says Cyrus, king of Persia: 'All the kingdoms of the earth the LORD, the God of heaven, has given to me, and he has also charged me to build him a house in Jerusalem, which is in Judah. 3Whoever, therefore, among you belongs to any part of his people, let him go up, and may his God be with him! 4Let everyone who has survived, in whatever place he may have dwelt, be assisted by the people of that place with silver, gold, goods, and cattle, together with free will offerings for the house of God in Jerusalem.'" 5Then the family heads of Judah and Benjamin and the priests and Levites—everyone, that is, whom God had inspired to do so—prepared to go up to build the house of the LORD in Jerusalem. 6All their neighbors gave them help in every way, with silver, gold, goods, and cattle, and with many precious gifts besides all their free-will offerings.

Less than fifty years after Nebuchadnezzar conquered much of the Fertile Crescent, another empire rose to power, from east of Babylon. Persia quickly gobbled up what once was Babylon's. The change of dominion brought more than just a change in leaders. Generous in victory, Cyrus, king of this newly expanded Persian Empire, desired to prove himself beneficent toward those whom Nebuchadnezzar had simply crushed. It was not uncommon for new rulers to be anxious to curry favor among their subjects upon coming into power. The Jews and many other peoples had experienced the obliterating might of Babylon. Cyrus, in conquering Babylon, saw a quick way to win the loyalty of those whom Babylon had conquered earlier. Return them to their homelands, let them build temples and pray for the prosperity of Cyrus and his empire.

Cyrus's decree, as recorded in both Ezra and at the end of 2 Chronicles, appears to assert Cyrus's personal identification of the God of Israel as the one behind his success as a conqueror, but Cyrus was more probably interested in winning the favor of as many of his subjects and as many of their gods as possible. Whatever Cyrus's motives were, we find in Isaiah the affirmation that the hand of God was directly responsible for Cyrus's decision.

A Prophecy

Isaiah 44:28

44:28I say of Cyrus: My shepherd,
who fulfills my every wish;
He shall say of Jerusalem, "Let her be rebuilt,"
and of the temple, "Let its foundations
be laid."

The words we find in Isaiah concerning the return of the exiles are from a prophet most commonly referred to by scholars as Second Isaiah. The Isaiah for whom the entire prophetic work is named lived during the reigns of Kings Uzziah (also known as Azariah) through Hezekiah of Judah and would have died long before the exile and over 160 years before Cyrus's decree telling them to return to

Judah. It was the task of prophets to warn God's people of future judgment and blessings, but always based on concerns for their present behavior, and never to peer so precisely into the future as to name names of world leaders two centuries ahead of time. Second Isaiah's prophetic career would have been sometime during the reign of Cyrus.

Even more telling, however, is the content of Isaiah 40–55 with its deep concern for God's people at the time of the exile and the exhortations and encouragement given them to return to Judah and recover their life as covenanted people in the land God had given them.

Decades of exile had taken a peculiar toll on the people of Judah. It was not enough to simply be told to go back home and rebuild the temple. After fifty years Babylon had become a very desirable home for many of the exiles. The people sent into exile were, in fact, the educated, the skilled artisans, and all those most likely to have talents useful to their captors. Over a few decades, many of the children and grandchildren of these people had probably become quite successful. Leaving for Jerusalem would mean abandoning a livelihood in one of the most advanced, bustling civilizations of the world for an abandoned city of ruins that would demand more muscle than brains to come back to life.

Prepare the Way of the Lord

Isaiah 40:1-4

> ⁴⁰:¹Comfort, give comfort to my people,
>   says your God.
> ²Speak tenderly to Jerusalem, and proclaim
>   to her
>   that her service is at an end,
>   her guilt is expiated;
> Indeed, she has received from the hand of
>   the LORD
>   double for all her sins.

> ³A voice cries out:
> In the desert prepare the way of the LORD!
>   Make straight in the wasteland a highway
>   for our God!
> ⁴Every valley shall be filled in,
>   every mountain and hill shall be made low;
> The rugged land shall be made a plain,
>   the rough country, a broad valley.

The comfort Isaiah announces for God's people is the good news that her exile is at an end. Whatever punishment was due them for their sins, what they have actually endured is double the measure. In verse 3, Christians hear a familiar voice cry out. It sounds remarkably like that of John the Baptist.

John Prepares the Way

Matthew 3:1-3

> ³:¹In those days John the Baptist appeared, preaching in the desert of Judea ²[and] saying, "Repent, for the kingdom of heaven is at hand!" ³It was of him that the prophet Isaiah had spoken when he said:
>   "A voice of one crying out in the desert,
>   'Prepare the way of the Lord,
>   make straight his paths.'"

Matthew, Mark (1:2-3), and Luke (3:2-6) all found in the Greek translation of the Old Testament known as the Septuagint a dramatic fulfillment of Isaiah's words in the preaching of John the Baptist. For them and for Christians ever since, the words of Isaiah are understood as proclaiming John the Baptist as the one who went into the wilderness to prepare a way for Christ to begin his ministry of salvation.

Knowing that these passages from Isaiah were first heard by exiled Jews in Babylon, however, should help us to gain an additional understanding. Scripture, in every generation, has the power to speak in fresh and powerful ways. This is what is known as the living word of God. Prophetic utterance, proclaimed once to a people in a particular historical circumstance, becomes engraved as Sacred Scripture and speaks anew to generation after generation. The words found in Isaiah 40:3-4 would come to bear new meaning in the appearance of John the Baptist. But when proclaimed to the Jews of the exile they had a very rich, distinct meaning for them.

Note that the Hebrew text of Isaiah is translated in most Bibles differently from the way the Greek is translated in the New Testament. The voice that cries out is not crying out in the desert (or wilderness). That translation fits John the Baptist all the better. But the Hebrew tells us simply that a voice cries out, telling the people to build a highway in the desert. The exiles are to find their way back to Jerusalem and the road they take should be straight and their way upon it steady, for the road is to be designed to fulfill the Lord's purpose: sending the people home!

These words also give us a hint of the challenge facing the prophet. The exiles are not lined up at a starting gate waiting for the word that will send them racing toward Jerusalem. The prophet has told them to begin the arduous task of making a highway through desert, valley, and mountains. They will not literally have to plow a road, but they will have to beat a broad path into the dry earth with their tired feet, either taking everything they own and hold dear with them or leaving it behind forever.

The work of getting to Jerusalem is only half the story. They are going to a city burned to the ground and strewn with rubble. If they are going to preserve their heritage as God's people they will have to build a temple. And if they are not to face the same threat of destruction all over again they will have to fortify the city and rebuild its walls.

Rebuilding the Temple

Haggai 1:1-11

1:1On the first day of the sixth month in the second year of King Darius, the word of the LORD came through the prophet Haggai to the governor of Judah, Zerubbabel, son of Shealtiel, and to the high priest Joshua, son of Jehozadak: 2Thus says the LORD of hosts: This people says: "Not now has the time come to rebuild the house of the LORD." 3(Then this word of the LORD came through Haggai, the prophet:) 4Is it time for you to dwell in your own paneled houses, while this house lies in ruins?

5Now thus says the LORD of hosts:
   Consider your ways!
6You have sown much, but have brought in little;
   you have eaten, but have not been satisfied;
You have drunk, but have not been exhilarated;
   have clothed yourselves, but not been warmed;
And he who earned wages
   earned them for a bag with holes in it.

7Thus says the LORD of hosts:
Consider your ways!
8Go up into the hill country;
   bring timber, and build the house
That I may take pleasure in it
   and receive my glory, says the LORD.
9You expected much, but it came to little;
   and what you brought home, I blew away.
For what cause? says the LORD of hosts.
   Because my house lies in ruins,
   while each of you hurries to his own house.
10Therefore the heavens withheld from you their dew,
   and the earth her crops.
11And I called for a drought
   upon the land and upon the mountains;
Upon the grain, and upon the wine, and
   upon the oil,

continue

> and upon all that the ground brings forth;
> Upon men and upon beasts,
> and upon all that is produced by hand.

Cyrus ordered the rebuilding of the temple in 538 BC. Darius succeeded him as emperor of the Persian empire and the date mentioned at the beginning of Haggai would have been 520 BC. Eighteen years have passed since the people began returning to Jerusalem, but the work of rebuilding the temple has apparently not yet begun.

The prophet Haggai is given a message from God to the governor of Judah, Zerubbabel, and to the high priest Joshua. We are also told a little of the family lineage of the governor and high priest so that informed readers will recognize their links to Judah's history. The governor is a descendant of David. We read in Zechariah 6:11-12 that there are high hopes that Zerubbabel may even be called king some day, but that day never comes. Matthew lists him as an ancestor of Joseph in Jesus' genealogy (1:12-13). Joshua is the high priest, a descendant of Aaron, Moses' brother. The importance of a high priest is founded on the duty of offering sacrifices in the temple. Since there is no temple, Haggai's exhortation to build one is directed at Judah's leaders.

In delivering God's message to the two most significant leaders of Judah, Haggai is clearly addressing all of Judah through them. His message to the former exiles is clear. Living solely for their own immediate gain, or simply for their daily sustenance, has left their lives meaningless and empty. They are apparently experiencing drought; perhaps they are close to famine. The prophet tells them that their labors have been for naught because they have declined to build the temple. Reward and punishment through natural events are still seen as a direct result of God's involvement in history. But the real theological insight is that as long as God is not given central importance in their lives, their lives are famished.

Zerubbabel laid the foundations of the temple in 520 BC, in apparent obedience to the Lord's command through Haggai and Zechariah. This second temple would be completed five years later.

Laying the Foundation

Ezra 3:12-13

3:12Many of the priests, Levites, and family heads, the old men who had seen the former house, cried out in sorrow as they watched the foundation of the present house being laid. Many others, however, lifted up their voices in shouts of joy, 13and no one could distinguish the sound of the joyful shouting from the sound of those who were weeping; for the people raised a mighty clamor which was heard afar off.

In Ezra the laying of the foundations of the second temple are met with mixed emotions. Those elderly folk who could remember Solomon's temple were reduced to tears, evidently because it was obvious that the new temple was going to be far less glorious than the first. Once the temple was completed, the city's walls had to be rebuilt, and this task was undertaken by Nehemiah, a layman and an attendant to the Persian emperor. After gaining permission to leave the royal court, he went to Jerusalem as its newly appointed governor (Neh 2:1-9).

Nehemiah's attempts to rebuild the walls were nearly frustrated by neighboring powers that warned succeeding emperors that a Jerusalem with protective walls would soon threaten the peace of the empire. Nehemiah's commission from the emperor Artaxerxes was put in writing and once the documents were produced, Nehemiah was able to complete his task. Judah would remain a vassal state, ruled not by its own king but by appointed governors. Its temple was a much more humble abode for God, but the pilgrimages of exile and return had thoroughly transformed the people of God.

The Scroll of the Law

Nehemiah 8:1-8

8:1Now when the seventh month came, the whole people gathered as one man in the open space before the Water Gate, and they called upon Ezra the scribe to bring forth the book of the law of Moses which the LORD prescribed for Israel. 2On the first day of the seventh month, therefore, Ezra the priest brought the law before the assembly, which consisted of men, women, and those children old enough to understand. 3Standing at one end of the open place that was before the Water Gate, he read out of the book from daybreak till midday, in the presence of the men, the women, and those children old enough to understand; and all the people listened attentively to the book of the law. 4Ezra the scribe stood on a wooden platform that had been made for the occasion; at his right side stood Mattithiah, Shema, Anaiah, Uriah, Hilkiah, and Maaseiah, and on his left Pedaiah, Mishael, Malchijah, Hashum, Hashbaddanah, Zechariah, Meshullam. 5Ezra opened the scroll so that all the people might see it (for he was standing higher up than any of the people); and, as he opened it, all the people rose. 6Ezra blessed the LORD, the great God, and all the people, their hands raised high, answered, "Amen, amen!" Then they bowed down and prostrated themselves before the LORD, their faces to the ground. 7[The Levites Jeshua, Bani, Sherebiah, Jamin, Akkub, Shabbethai, Hodiah, Maaseiah, Kelita, Azariah, Jozabad, Hanan, and Pelaiah explained the law to the people, who remained in their places.] 8Ezra read plainly from the book of the law of God, interpreting it so that all could understand what was read.

There is a lack of certainty among scholars as to the exact timeline between Ezra and Nehemiah. Some believe Nehemiah actually arrived in Jerusalem first, even though the biblical texts are set up to show Ezra arriving first. This should not distract us from the great significance to Judaism of both Ezra and Nehemiah. Ezra is both a priest and a scribe, while Nehemiah is a layman. They are depicted as working together for the building up of God's people, each using their positions of authority (Ezra's is religious, Nehemiah's is secular) to complement each others' labors.

Because of Ezra, the people will come to understand clearly how to live as a people covenanted to God. Because of Nehemiah, the people will be able to live securely in the land. Ezra's role marks something distinctive in the faith of Judah's people. This moment when Ezra proclaims the law of Moses and has it interpreted for the people of Judah is so distinctive that many scholars see it as the first moment when Israelite religion actually becomes what we know as Judaism.

This might raise some eyebrows. If Judaism began when Ezra proclaimed and interpreted Moses' law to the people who had returned to Judah from the exile, what religion were they before that moment? To be precise, it needs to be explained that marking this moment as the beginning of Judaism does not mean the people changed religions, but it does indicate that their religion underwent a profound change. When Ezra, both a priest and a scribe, reads and interprets the law to the people, the religion of Judah becomes a religion in which the Torah (the Pentateuch, or law of Moses) becomes of central concern to the practice of their faith. It is Ezra's function as a scribe that gets the most attention in Scripture, not his status as a priest.

Before the exile, worship of YHWH in Jerusalem's temple was the most distinctive feature of Judah's religion. Scholars frequently refer to this stage in the people's faith as Yahwism. With the destruction of the temple and their exile from their homeland, however, the religious leaders acted with passion and dedication to preserve the faith and history of their people. One of the most significant things they did was to gather together many of the oral and written traditions of Israel and Judah and to compile a definitive written version of the law ascribed to Moses.

When the people returned to Judah, they had to be thoroughly reacquainted with their faith, their traditions, and their history as God's people. The texts arranged and compiled during the exile would greatly help in this matter, but these were all written in Hebrew, a language belonging to an earlier people.

The people cannot understand their covenant with God without someone to interpret for them. When the people were driven into Babylon their language was Hebrew. When they came back it was a different, though related, language known as Aramaic. Outside of the study of the Torah, which was written in Hebrew, Aramaic became the language of the Jewish people right up through the life of Christ and until the destruction of the last temple in AD 70. Proclaiming and interpreting the Word of God is the task of a scribe, and so Ezra's role as a scribe becomes paramount.

A new temple is built and dedicated, and sacrificial worship of YHWH is renewed there. But from now on, the religion of the people will become more and more centered on ethical and ritual observance of Moses' law as interpreted by scribes and applied to daily living. This will be true in part because so many Jews will never return to Jerusalem. Whether by choice or necessity, they will attempt to live faithful lives far from the temple in whatever lands they have settled in. Scripture and its authoritative interpretation will be the guiding light of their faith.

Ezra read to the assembled people "from **the book of the law of God**" (Neh 8:8), which in Hebrew is the *torah* (literally "direction, instruction, law"). Scholars generally agree that Ezra was reading from the legal material contained in the first five books of the Old Testament, or the *Pentateuch* (literally "five books" or "five scrolls").

Another Exile

Matthew 2:13b-21

²:¹³[T]he angel of the Lord appeared to Joseph in a dream and said, "Rise, take the child and his mother, flee to Egypt, and stay there until I tell you. Herod is going to search for the child to destroy him." ¹⁴Joseph rose and took the child and his mother by night and departed for Egypt. ¹⁵He stayed there until the death of Herod, that what the Lord had said through the prophet might be fulfilled, "Out of Egypt I called my son."

¹⁶When Herod realized that he had been deceived by the magi, he became furious. He ordered the massacre of all the boys in Bethlehem and its vicinity two years old and under, in accordance with the time he had ascertained from the magi. ¹⁷Then was fulfilled what had been said through Jeremiah the prophet:

¹⁸"A voice was heard in Ramah,
  sobbing and loud lamentation;
Rachel weeping for her children,
  and she would not be consoled,
  since they were no more."

¹⁹When Herod had died, behold, the angel of the Lord appeared in a dream to Joseph in Egypt ²⁰and said, "Rise, take the child and his mother and go to the land of Israel, for those who sought the child's life are dead." ²¹He rose, took the child and his mother, and went to the land of Israel.

The account of the Holy Family's flight to Egypt entails a jump of many centuries from the time of Ezra and Nehemiah. It is not too big a jump, however, because it is a story of a Jewish family who must flee their homeland and endure exile in Egypt like the prophet Jeremiah (Jer 43:4-7) and so many Jewish families before them. The irony, however, is that Joseph, Mary, and their infant child are fleeing for safety from a supposedly Jewish king.

The Herod of Jesus' infancy is referred to as Herod the Great by many historians, but not because of any hint of goodness. He was Herod the Great because his skillful use of power and his willingness to kill any opponent, including wives or children if they even hinted disloyalty, made this greatly feared ruler stand out from any of his descendants who also bore the name Herod. His identity as a Jew is a slender one. His father was an Idumean, a people who had been forcibly converted to Judaism and not wholly accepted by other Jews. His mother was Arabian. Nevertheless, history and a great deal of intrigue conspired to make Rome recognize Herod as "King of the Jews."

An astute and often brutal leader, he was "king" only inasmuch as he could keep Rome happy. The Jewish people he governed, however, hated Roman occupation and the desire to revolt was always simmering. Herod was adept at placating these irreconcilable forces. To the Romans he continually demonstrated his love for all things associated with Hellenism, for Greek cultural influence was still the glue that held much of the Roman Empire together. To his people, however, Herod publicly displayed himself as an observant Jew. Among his many building projects, he launched the renovation of Jerusalem's temple that would be continued long after his death. His plans for the temple could be regarded as a lavish and artful ploy to gain the support of many influential Jews.

In addition to the temple in Jerusalem, Herod also built a temple in Samaria to honor Octavian, otherwise known as Caesar Augustus.

He is one of only a few biblical characters from the New Testament whose place in history is so well documented that there is no problem affixing precise dates to his life. He reigned from 37–4 BC, which is one of the reasons historians are fairly certain that our calendars are off by as many as six years. For Herod to have been king when Jesus was born, Jesus had to have been born no later than 4 BC. A date of 6–4 BC for Jesus' birth is tentatively given by most scholars.

Only in Matthew do we find the account of the Holy Family's flight to Egypt, and nowhere outside of this account do we have any record of Herod slaying the infant boys in the region of Bethlehem. Many historians are quick to note, however, that such a heinous act was perfectly in keeping with Herod's character.

One of the prominent characteristics of Matthew's gospel is its portrayal of Jesus as the ideal Israel. Through the prophet Hosea, God refers to Israel as his son and reminds Israel that it was God who brought Israel into that special relationship by delivering the Israelites from slavery in Egypt (Hos 11:1). Matthew is certain that Jesus brings a special meaning to Hosea's prophetic words when Joseph and Mary bring him out of Egypt and return with him to Palestine. Jesus is God's Son; he is also the embodiment of faithful Israel.

With just a few words, Matthew is able to imbed in Christian faith the epic nature of this panicked flight to Egypt and their still-fearful return to their homeland. Matthew is an extremely skillful theologian. By connecting the flight to Egypt and the return to the Promised Land to the words of the prophet Hosea, Matthew taps the entire history of Israel, from the Exodus to the exile and return, and places all the hopes of Israel for redemption from its past failures to live up to God's expectations in this one small child, Jesus. This is a pilgrimage that is meant to transform those who read of it into faithful followers!

We would miss something significant, however, if we dwelt only on the epic proportions of the flight to Egypt, for it is, after all, also an account of a poor family with meager resources fleeing their homeland out of fear for their child's life. It is in Matthew's gospel that Jesus most clearly tells us that our reception of the poor, the young, and the needy is the measure of our reception of Jesus (18:5; 25:31-45). The account of the Holy Family's flight to Egypt becomes for us, then, a reminder of the shared identity with Christ found in families and individuals all over the world who are forced into desperate flights from their homes as a matter of survival.

It is fitting then, in a Christian examination of Israel's painful pilgrimages of exile and return, that we find so much of Israel's story encapsulated by Matthew in this pilgrimage of the infant Jesus, the one our faith proclaims as the Jewish Messiah. In the next (and final) chapter, following Jesus will define for us the very heart of the Christian pilgrimage of faith, a pilgrimage that can also be described as discipleship.

EXPLORING LESSON THREE

1. How would you describe the difference between the *goal* of a pilgrimage and the *purpose* of a pilgrimage?

   goal - to get somewhere

   purpose - to learn from it / some sort of transformation

2. In what ways do the demands of a physical pilgrimage reflect the challenges we experience in our lifelong spiritual pilgrimage of faith?

3. From a religious perspective, what was especially traumatic about the conquest and exile experienced by the people of the northern kingdom and the kingdom of Judah?

   Asirians   Babylonians

   - felt that God was abandoning them
   - I must have done something wrong

4. a) The fate of the Israelites, who became homeless exiles as the result of a military conflict, has been shared by countless peoples up to the present day. What challenges to faith do forced migrations caused by war, ethnic cleansing, or religious oppression pose for those who experience them?

   b) How might families fleeing danger today find comfort in the plight of the Holy Family, who were also refugees (Matt 2:13-23)?

5. What memories or reflections may have sustained the faith of Jewish believers during the almost fifty years of their exile in Babylon?

_____

_____

_____

_____

6. a) Why might Cyrus's decree, which ended the Babylonian captivity and allowed the Jewish people to return to their homeland (Ezra 1:1-4), have presented a dilemma for some of the exiles and their families?

_____

_____

_____

_____

   b) Have you ever struggled to make a decision when circumstances made it difficult to accept something good?

_____

_____

_____

_____

7. How does knowledge of the original context of Isaiah 40:3 enhance and deepen your appreciation of references to that verse in Matthew 3:1-3, Mark 1:2-3, and Luke 3:2-6?

_____

_____

_____

_____

8. Why are the prophet Haggai's words directed to Zerubbabel and Joshua (Hag 1:1)? What are their roles, and why are those roles so important in the temple rebuilding effort?

_____

_____

_____

_____

9. The reading of the book of the law by Ezra (Neh 8:1-8) is seen by many scholars as a pivotal moment in the transformation of the religion of the Israelites. What distinguishes the form Judaism took after that event from the practice which had preceded it?

_____

_____

_____

_____

10. The Gospel of Matthew portrays Jesus as the ideal Israel, beginning with the reference to Hosea 11:1 in Matthew 2:15. What theological point is the evangelist making by including this reference in his narrative?

_____

_____

_____

_____

CLOSING PRAYER

Prayer

*I rejoiced when they said to me,
  "Let us go to the house of the Lord."
And now our feet are standing
  within your gates, Jerusalem.* (Ps 122:1-2)

Lord God, in days long past your chosen people made joyful pilgrimage to offer sacrifice and prayers in your temple at Jerusalem. Inspire us, we pray, with the same spirit of jubilation as we make our way to worship you. May the peace, prosperity, and love for which our ancestors in faith prayed be ours, and may we always be grateful for the good things you have given us. This day we pray in gratitude for the blessings of . . .

LESSON FOUR

Come, Follow Me

Begin your personal study and group discussion with a simple and sincere prayer such as:

Prayer

God, you are the source and goal of all life. Strengthen, support, and guide us on our earthly pilgrimage so that, nourished by your word and inspired by your Son's example, we may persevere in faith until we find ourselves home at last in your heavenly kingdom.

Read pages 68–80, Lesson Four.

Respond to the questions on pages 81–83, Exploring Lesson Four.

The Closing Prayer on page 83 is for your personal use and may be used at the end of group discussion.

COME, FOLLOW ME

The Visitation

Luke 1:39-45

^{1:39}During those days Mary set out and traveled to the hill country in haste to a town of Judah, ⁴⁰where she entered the house of Zechariah and greeted Elizabeth. ⁴¹When Elizabeth heard Mary's greeting, the infant leaped in her womb, and Elizabeth, filled with the holy Spirit, ⁴²cried out in a loud voice and said, "Most blessed are you among women, and blessed is the fruit of your womb. ⁴³And how does this happen to me, that the mother of my Lord should come to me? ⁴⁴For at the moment the sound of your greeting reached my ears, the infant in my womb leaped for joy. ⁴⁵Blessed are you who believed that what was spoken to you by the Lord would be fulfilled."

Mary has learned from the angel Gabriel that Elizabeth, her kinswoman of mature age, is with child. Perhaps Elizabeth's age is reason enough for Mary to set out in haste to visit her. Elizabeth would want someone young and capable to help her during the last months of her pregnancy.

Mary may also have had her personal reasons. She is a very young woman, only just of age to be betrothed. It is commonly speculated that she is in her early teens when she learns that she herself is to miraculously conceive a child, one who will be called the Son of God. Since her marriage to Joseph is only a pending reality, this pregnancy is hardly news she would have eagerly shared with neighbors and friends. It could well be that Mary needs and wants someone to confide in, someone who knows that these things can come about following the word of an angel.

Raymond Brown, the late biblical scholar who wrote with great expertise on the infancy narratives, contends that when Gabriel announced Elizabeth's pregnancy to Mary, she would have understood it as a divine imperative. She was under orders from God to visit Elizabeth, and being completely faithful, Mary goes to her cousin in haste.

What is not said about Mary's journey is that she would not have undertaken it on her own. She is young, she is female, and the journey is into the hill country outside of Jerusalem, a considerable distance from Nazareth. Tradition names Ain Karem, just southwest of Jerusalem, where modern pilgrims will find the Church of the Visitation and the Church of the Nativity of St. John, among others. We know nothing about Mary's chaperones; Luke's narrative is concerned with other matters.

This story of a divinely directed encounter of two women, both miraculously pregnant, definitely has more to it than what appears on the surface. Mary greets Elizabeth, and Elizabeth greets her in return, adding a joyful blessing. The women are the ones we hear from, but the real greeting has taken place at a deeper level. Luke knows his readers may have lingering questions about the relative status of John and Jesus, and this narrative lets us see and hear who is greater and who is lesser without bombast or preaching.

Within Elizabeth's womb, the unborn prophet John has sensed the one that John is destined to proclaim as his greater. We often note that persons of greatness in history had a destiny, that they were "born" to be someone of great significance. John is not even born yet, but he already knows his purpose. Sensing the presence of the Messiah nestled embryonically within the one whose voice has greeted his own mother, John cannot contain his joy. He leaps in Elizabeth's womb and his joy floods through so that even she cannot help but share it.

Mary's journey to her cousin's home has given us a peek at the path that each child will go down when the time is ripe for revelation. John will call the people of Israel to repentance in the waters of the Jordan, and the people will wonder if he is the one for whom they have all been waiting. But John will sense in Jesus one who is even greater than he.

 Of the four gospels, Luke gives the most attention to **Mary**. Artists throughout history have portrayed poignant scenes from Luke's infancy narrative (chapters 1–2) such as the annunciation and the visitation. Mary takes center stage throughout the story as it unfolds and her destiny to be the mother of Jesus is revealed. Mary expresses her response to God's mysterious will in the Canticle of Mary, which she speaks during her encounter with Elizabeth when both women are pregnant (Luke 1:46-55). Filled with Old Testament imagery, this beautiful hymn shows that Mary acquiesces totally to God's will, even without understanding it fully: "The Mighty One has done great things for me, / and holy is his name" (1:49).

The Beginning of the Gospel

Mark 1:1-18

¹:¹The beginning of the gospel of Jesus Christ [the Son of God].

²As it is written in Isaiah the prophet:

"Behold, I am sending my messenger ahead of you;
    he will prepare your way.
³A voice of one crying out in the desert:
    'Prepare the way of the Lord,
        make straight his paths.'"

⁴John [the] Baptist appeared in the desert proclaiming a baptism of repentance for the forgiveness of sins. ⁵People of the whole Judean countryside and all the inhabitants of Jerusalem were going out to him and were being baptized by him in the Jordan River as they acknowledged their sins. ⁶John was clothed in camel's hair, with a leather belt around his waist. He fed on locusts and wild honey. ⁷And this is what he proclaimed: "One mightier than I is coming after me. I am not worthy to stoop and loosen the thongs of his sandals. ⁸I have baptized you with water; he will baptize you with the holy Spirit."

⁹It happened in those days that Jesus came from Nazareth of Galilee and was baptized in the Jordan by John. ¹⁰On coming up out of the water he saw the heavens being torn open and the Spirit, like a dove, descending upon him. ¹¹And a voice came from the heavens, "You are my beloved Son; with you I am well pleased."

¹²At once the Spirit drove him out into the desert, ¹³and he remained in the desert for forty days, tempted by Satan. He was among wild beasts, and the angels ministered to him.

¹⁴After John had been arrested, Jesus came to Galilee proclaiming the gospel of God: ¹⁵"This is the time of fulfillment. The kingdom of God is at hand. Repent, and believe in the gospel."

¹⁶As he passed by the Sea of Galilee, he saw Simon and his brother Andrew casting their nets into the sea; they were fishermen. ¹⁷Jesus said to them, "Come after me, and I will make you fishers of men." ¹⁸Then they abandoned their nets and followed him.

When you open your New Testament to the second gospel, it is usually titled "The Gospel according to Mark." Mark himself had another title in mind. He called it, "the beginning of the gospel of Jesus Christ" (Mark 1:1). Sometimes we read this first verse in Mark as simply a prelude to the opening chapter, as though Mark needs to point out that these verses are the beginning of his gospel. But recently some very astute scholars have come to the conclusion that Mark considered his whole gospel as just the beginning of the Good News about Jesus Christ.

Mark was the first gospel written, so it was indeed just the beginning of the gospels, but Mark is not alerting us to the fact that he is writing the first gospel. As a title, the opening verse of Mark really suggests that the good news of Jesus Christ, the Son of God, is just beginning for us when we, after reading his gospel, can profess our own faith that Jesus *is* the Christ, the Son of God. This is a faithful beginning, but our faith must take us somewhere. For Mark, that somewhere is Calvary. We begin our life of faith by believing, but our believing requires us to accept the cross that Jesus refused to shrug. Our believing in Jesus will reveal to us a cross that we too must bear (Mark 8:34).

 The word **"gospel"**—from the Old English *godspel*, or "good tidings"—is now most commonly used to describe the accounts of Jesus' life and teachings written by the four evangelists (Matthew, Mark, Luke, and John). The word "gospel" may also signify, as in the letters of Paul, not a particular narrative of Jesus' life but rather the *meaning* of his life, death, and resurrection for us. In Paul's letters, "gospel" refers to the "good news" that by his death and resurrection Jesus has opened a way, through faith, by which all can be justified and saved. Indeed, the centerpiece of Jesus' own preaching ministry was the "good news" or the "gospel" that "the kingdom of God is at hand" (Mark 1:14-15).

Mark wrote in a time of persecution, and so he wants those who profess to believe in

Jesus to fully understand that believing in Jesus means accepting a costly discipleship. Mark also knows that this was never an easy message to sell. As in no other gospel, Mark shows how resistant Peter and the rest of the twelve were to the message of the cross. By including sharp rebukes from Jesus, Mark warns that failure to understand the cross is a failure to understand who Jesus is (8:31-33).

Along with the importance of the word "beginning" in the first verse of Mark, noted New Testament scholar Brendan Byrne also stresses the importance of the word "gospel." Today, we naturally associate "gospel" with the good news of salvation found in Jesus Christ. There were other overtones to the word that Mark's first hearers would have associated with "gospel," however. The word evoked prophetic messages found in Isaiah (52:7):

> How beautiful upon the mountains
>   are the feet of him who brings glad tidings,
> Announcing peace, bearing good news,
>   announcing salvation, and saying to Zion,
>   "Your God is King!"

This prophetic message had strong political overtones. Announcing to Zion that their God is King was a way of promising that the foreign dominion over Israel and its people was going to be replaced by God's own rule.

Many other scholars have also noted that even in the secular world, "gospel" had a definite meaning in Mark's time that would not have been lost on his audience. The emperor Caesar Augustus had his reign published as a "gospel" throughout the Roman Empire. He wanted everyone to recognize his rule as "good news" that promised peace and prosperity, as long as no one offered resistance.

When Mark announces his document as "the beginning of the gospel of Jesus Christ," he is claiming that Jesus Christ is central to an act of ultimate liberation that was both God's doing and had consequences for the whole world, not just Israel. God's call, which we have traced from the call of Abraham and Sarah, is now a call to the whole world. While Mark may only hint at the call to the wider world, the majority opinion is that Mark wrote his gospel for Roman Christians, and the hints would not have been lost on his mostly Gentile audience.

The second verse of Mark informs us of the importance of the ministry of John the Baptist in launching Jesus' own ministry. John's baptism is introduced through a complex quotation from the Old Testament, a combination of phrases from Malachi, Isaiah, and Exodus, which are meant to sum up the expectation created by (Second) Isaiah of God's full promises to Israel following the Babylonian exile. In Isaiah 40:3, the call to "prepare the way of the LORD" actually involves a call to the exiles in Babylon to get on the road and return to Jerusalem. As employed in Mark, it is to alert us to John's ministry of baptism in the Jordan. John is preparing a way for the Lord to enter the lives of the people. And the Lord coming to them is Jesus the Christ. The journey that will transform all who respond to it in faith is the journey that God, in Jesus, undertakes in order to be the good news of God's salvation.

John's preaching draws the people from their homes and they follow him into the Jordan to receive a baptism of repentance. Many Jews of the time took ritual baths in moving water in order to make themselves "pure" again in a religious sense. These ritual baths may have something to do with John and his practice of baptism. Ritual baths were almost routine among some sects of Judaism. The Essenes of Qumran (a wilderness area near the Dead Sea) had an elaborate watering system installed with a pool designed for regular use by the adherents of their community. While some have speculated that John may have been influenced, even deeply influenced, by the Qumran community, John's baptism in the Jordan wasn't a ritual intended to be repeated time and again by those who heard his message.

Crossing through the Jordan River was how Israel understood its birth as a nation. Even as Moses had led the people of Israel through the waters of a sea (Exod 14:10-22), after forty years of wandering in the wilderness, Joshua finally led Israel into the land of their inheritance by crossing through the waters of the Jordan (Josh 3:14-17). By baptizing the people in the Jordan, John was calling on them to renew themselves as a nation. Many scholars would go further and say that John was hoping to identify the eschatological people of God, that is, the people of a new Israel that would be worthy of the Messiah at his coming, which John would have associated with the end of time.

 Eschatology refers to the study of the "last things" affecting either an individual or all of creation. Traditionally, these "last things" have been identified as death, judgment, heaven, and hell. In theological usage, "eschatology" can refer to the expectations of God's people for the "end of the age" or the end of human history—expectations that include God's final triumph over evil and God's final deliverance of his people.

"The way of the Lord" is a path both for the Lord to come to Israel as well as a path for Israel to come to the Lord. It is John who is depicted as the voice in the wilderness, and so we are to understand that John's divinely appointed purpose is to make the Lord Jesus known to Israel. John does this by preparing the people to welcome their Lord through a baptism of repentance. Jesus the Lord is revealed after undergoing the same baptism of repentance as Israel. Mark in no way wants us to think Jesus is in personal need of such a baptism, but Jesus does represent Israel. Jesus is the Lord who will bring Israel's God back to the people, a people who are oppressed not just by Rome but by the devil, the very personification of evil. Jesus' first act of restoring Israel's life with God is performed by entering the waters of baptism, defining "the way" for Israel to return to the Lord.

Upon coming out of the waters, the Spirit descends on Jesus and Mark's readers become privy to a moment of intimacy between Father and Son. The Father directly addresses Jesus:

"You are my beloved Son; with you I am well pleased" (1:11). No human will confirm what God has just revealed in Jesus' baptism until the centurion beholds his death upon the cross (15:39). We have to stay with the entire Gospel of Mark before anyone understands who Jesus is; such is the pilgrimage of faith that Mark invites us to personally undertake. Mark seems well aware that we will eagerly claim our faith in Jesus, even showering him with titles like "Lord," "Messiah," and "Son of David." What Mark wants to teach us is that if we are to embrace him as "Son of God," we must also embrace the cross.

Jesus loses no time in accepting his mission. As soon as we learn that the Spirit has come upon Jesus, we also learn that the Spirit drives him into the wilderness to face a direct confrontation with personal evil. This evil, joined with religious and political opposition, will eventually nail him to a cross.

Jesus is tempted by the devil in the wilderness. Mark leaves out all the details found in Matthew 4 and Luke 4, but his message is clear. Just as Israel was tested in the wilderness for forty years, Jesus endures forty days of temptation. Unlike Israel, however, there are no failures. Whether the wild beasts are meant to be seen as an additional threat to Jesus during his period of testing, or are presented as a sign of the messianic age he is inaugurating ("Then the wolf shall be a guest of the lamb, / and the leopard shall lie down with the kid." Isa 11:6) isn't clear. Either way, it points to Jesus' special success in circumstances where God's people had previously failed.

How much time elapses between Jesus' temptation in the wilderness and John the Baptist's arrest? Mark offers no suggestion; he presents the moment when Jesus begins his proclamation of the gospel as something that succeeds John's mission both in time and in importance: "This is the time of fulfillment. The kingdom of God is at hand. Repent, and believe in the gospel" (1:15).

The gospel Jesus proclaims is the good news that the kingdom of God is at hand. This is the time when the promises of God to Israel found in the words of the prophets and recorded in Scripture are to be fulfilled. It is perhaps the excitement that such a proclamation would produce among people yearning for the day of Israel's liberation and the return of God's abundant blessings that draws the attention of Andrew and Simon (1:16-18). This is something worthy of dropping your fishing nets for (Simon and Andrew) or abandoning your boat over (John and James, see Mark 1:19-20).

Many in Mark, including Peter and the disciples, are eager to see in Jesus an answer to woes both personal and national. Little wonder, then, that as Jesus reveals more and more about how the Scriptures are to be fulfilled (see 14:41-49), his disciples refuse to accept that the good news of the kingdom could entail anything so horrible as the crucifixion. Throughout Mark, the disciples are unwilling to associate a cruel death on a Roman cross with their faith in Jesus. But, step by step, Mark assures us that it is the cross that actually reveals Jesus' identity as the Son of God.

Staying with Jesus

John 1:35-39a

> [1:35]The next day John was there again with two of his disciples, [36]and as he watched Jesus walk by, he said, "Behold, the Lamb of God." [37]The two disciples heard what he said and followed Jesus. [38]Jesus turned and saw them following him and said to them, "What are you looking for?" They said to him, "Rabbi" (which translated means Teacher), "where are you staying?" [39]He said to them, "Come, and you will see." So they went and saw where he was staying, and they stayed with him that day.

In the Gospel of John we never actually read that John baptized Jesus. We are only told that John witnessed the Spirit descending on Jesus and that John knew that was the sign marking Jesus as the one John the Baptist was himself waiting for, the one whose sandal strap he was unworthy to untie (1:19-34). The Gospel of John is very careful never to suggest that Jesus at any point actually submitted himself in some way to John the Baptist. When we analyze Jesus' relationship to John in each of the four gospels, we discover that they all take special care to emphasize that John recognized Jesus' greater status. There may have been a time when Jesus helped John in his ministry, leaving the impression with some that John was the master and Jesus was the disciple.

At some point after witnessing the Spirit's descent upon Jesus, he sees Jesus and alerts two of his own disciples to the presence of the one whose rank greatly surpasses his own ("Behold, the Lamb of God"). These two former disciples of John immediately go to Jesus and ask where he is staying. It is a bit of a twist from what we usually think of as the calling of the disciples. Here, Jesus doesn't call them at all. John the Baptist points out Jesus to two of his own disciples (one of them is Andrew and the other is probably the beloved disciple, who remains unnamed throughout the gospel), and those two seek Jesus out.

But Jesus actually does invite them to discipleship in a manner that is key to the way the Gospel of John describes discipleship. The two who have, up until now, been disciples of John the Baptist, ask Jesus where he is staying. Jesus tells them to "come and see." They are being invited to follow him, and in following him they will become witnesses to where Jesus is "staying." The word for "staying" is the same word used throughout the Gospel of John for "remaining," or, as in many translations, "abiding." In John 15:4, we hear from Jesus that discipleship is a matter of "remaining" or "abiding" in Jesus.

"Remain in me, as I remain in you. Just as a branch cannot bear fruit on its own unless it remains on the vine, so neither can you unless you remain in me."

John's gospel doesn't tell us where Jesus was abiding when these two chose to stay with him.

But they did "stay" with him, and from then on, they became Jesus' disciples, not John the Baptist's. It could be important that the place where Jesus was staying is not named. In John's gospel, Jesus truly remains not in a physical place, but in the Father's love (15:10). At last, our quest to understand the theme of pilgrimage can take a short rest. Instead of endlessly roaming and wandering, we can now understand our calling as one of remaining and abiding.

Wherever it was, this nameless place where Jesus was physically staying, it becomes the site where Andrew introduces his brother Peter to Jesus. Very quickly Jesus has three disciples and on the very next day they go to Galilee, where Jesus finds Philip. In Jesus' call to Philip, we first hear the words in John to "follow me." Just as Andrew introduced Peter to Jesus, Philip attempts to introduce Nathanael to Jesus. But Jesus has already seen Nathanael and his insight into Nathanael's soul calls Nathanael into becoming a disciple.

Taking up the Cross

Mark 8:34-38

8:34He summoned the crowd with his disciples and said to them, "Whoever wishes to come after me must deny himself, take up his cross, and follow me. 35For whoever wishes to save his life will lose it, but whoever loses his life for my sake and that of the gospel will save it. 36What profit is there for one to gain the whole world and forfeit his life? 37What could one give in exchange for his life? 38Whoever is ashamed of me and of my words in this faithless and sinful generation, the Son of Man will be ashamed of when he comes in his Father's glory with the holy angels."

Jesus demands that we all take up our cross if we are to be his followers, and the call to follow Jesus is directed to every one of the baptized. We probably will not be asked to die for the faith, but our living and our dying is something we are called to do in the context of our faith. As Paul put it in his letter to the Romans (14:7-8):

> None of us lives for oneself, and no one dies for oneself. For if we live, we live for the Lord, and if we die, we die for the Lord; so then, whether we live or die, we are the Lord's.

The cross we are called to bear will, at the very least, become evident in the challenge to be faithful to Jesus' teaching as we live our day-to-day lives. Whatever extraordinary circumstances we may be called to endure with faith, if we are conscious of our calling as Christians, the reality of the cross will always be somewhere in our conscience.

Burying the Dead

Matthew 8:18-22

8:18When Jesus saw a crowd around him, he gave orders to cross to the other side. 19A scribe approached and said to him, "Teacher, I will follow you wherever you go." 20Jesus answered him, "Foxes have dens and birds of the sky have nests, but the Son of Man has nowhere to rest his head." 21Another of [his] disciples said to him, "Lord, let me go first and bury my father." 22But Jesus answered him, "Follow me, and let the dead bury their dead."

We have seen how John treats the place where Jesus abides. In Matthew, the call to discipleship clearly warns would-be disciples that they will be leaving home and family in order to follow Jesus. All the creatures of the earth have a home, but not the "Son of Man."

The title "Son of Man" can have more than one meaning in the gospels. It might pointedly refer to Jesus as a messianic figure in light of how some people would have read Daniel 7:13.

In the tradition of Ezekiel, however, the phrase "son of man" seems to mean no more than an accentuation of the fact that Ezekiel is human, a mortal of fragile flesh and blood, in relationship to God who is anything but mortal. Here in Matthew, there might be a sense of both meanings all at once. All the creatures of the earth have a home, but not this creature of flesh and blood. This "Son of Man" is the one figure on the face of the earth for whom it makes sense to leave everything else behind.

Is this call to follow Jesus a little too harsh? Does demanding that the dead bury their dead leave all worldly concerns for loved ones in the realm of "secular," unchristian behavior? It seems quite evident that Jesus allowed no excuses to come between a decision to follow him or to spend one's life doing something else. It is important, however, to recognize that the one who asked to go and bury his father is already called one of his disciples (v. 21). This would suggest that one who had already accepted the call to follow Jesus now wanted to leave in order to bury his father.

What is also likely is that he wasn't simply asking for a few days off in order to attend a funeral. The request to bury his father most likely meant he would like to go home with the option of resuming discipleship after his father, who might be quite healthy and robust for years to come, had died. The request was to make family obligations paramount over the obligation of a disciple to follow Jesus. Those of us who have families rightly regard our duty toward family as a Christian commitment, a sacrament, in fact, when our family includes a spouse. For most of us, following Christ is most likely to mean not just honoring our obligations to family but also serving the spiritual and physical well-being of our families above and beyond what is strictly expected of us. Following Jesus, however, is always absolute. If there is ever a question of whether we should follow Jesus or follow some other obligation, we are to follow Jesus.

The "dead" of this world, to whom Jesus refers, are those who cannot hear the call. They are those for whom all obligations begin and end with concerns that have no spiritual horizons, no purpose greater than what their eyes can see or their hands can touch. They are already dead, so let them attend to their dead. We know from every gospel's depiction of the love and concern shown by Joseph of Arimathea and the women who went to Jesus' tomb to anoint his body after his death that care and concern for the dead has tremendous spiritual value (Matt 27:57-61; 28:1; Mark 15:42–16:2; Luke 23:50–24:1; John 19:38–20:1).

Go and Proclaim the Kingdom

Matthew 10:5-10

> 10:5Jesus sent out these twelve after instructing them thus, "Do not go into pagan territory or enter a Samaritan town. 6Go rather to the lost sheep of the house of Israel. 7As you go, make this proclamation: 'The kingdom of heaven is at hand.' 8Cure the sick, raise the dead, cleanse lepers, drive out demons. Without cost you have received; without cost you are to give. 9Do not take gold or silver or copper for your belts; 10no sack for the journey, or a second tunic, or sandals, or walking stick. The laborer deserves his keep."

Jesus had very specific instructions for the Twelve. After the resurrection they will be told to go into the whole world, but during his ministry, Jesus sent them out as an extension of his own ministry to "the lost sheep of the house of Israel." His ministry is focused on Israel because it is a manifestation of God's faithfulness to the covenant with Israel. The message at the heart of Jesus' ministry is the same one he commands the Twelve to proclaim: "The kingdom of heaven is at hand." What Matthew usually calls "the kingdom of heaven" is referred to as "the kingdom of God" in Mark and Luke. The proclamation of the nearness of the kingdom of heaven was not a message about how to get to heaven, but both a warning and a promise that the rule of God was about to be asserted on earth, and in Israel in particular.

That God was about to reign might have had several connotations for the people who heard it. Certainly, it would mean an end to oppression and injustice. What Jesus thought it meant can be discerned by what he tells the Twelve they must do in confirmation of the message that the kingdom was close at hand (in other words, so close you can almost touch it). The sick are to be cured, the dead raised to new life, leapers cleansed (meaning that they were not just healed, but restored to full life within the community), and demons, the power of personal evil, were to be put to flight.

We often forget that the message of the kingdom was to be accompanied by demonstrations of its nearness. Pilgrims of faith are not simply people wandering the earth waiting for a happy homeland in heaven. They are followers of Christ, the Christ who went into the world with all its ills and made the hope extended by a living, loving God a personal reality in the lives of those who suffer. Those who are touched by the presence of God in this life will truly live in hope of the fullness of God's presence in the life to come. All Christians are sent into the world to communicate this reality in whatever way they are gifted.

The Transfiguration

Luke 9:28b-33, 51-52a

> 9:28[H]e took Peter, John, and James and went up the mountain to pray. 29While he was praying his face changed in appearance and his clothing became dazzling white. 30And behold, two men were conversing with him, Moses and Elijah, 31who appeared in glory and spoke of his exodus that he was going to accomplish in Jerusalem. 32Peter and his companions had been overcome
> *continue*

by sleep, but becoming fully awake, they saw his glory and the two men standing with him. [33]As they were about to part from him, Peter said to Jesus, "Master, it is good that we are here; let us make three tents, one for you, one for Moses, and one for Elijah." But he did not know what he was saying. . . .

[51]When the days for his being taken up were fulfilled, he resolutely determined to journey to Jerusalem, [52]and he sent messengers ahead of him.

The kingdom of God is made known through action, through deeds of healing and liberation from evil. Prayer, however, is the circumstance that reveals Jesus' glory. This special insight into the transfiguration is emphasized only in Luke. He is also alone in emphasizing the content of Jesus' conversation with Moses and Elijah. In doing so, Luke sums up the teaching of all the Law and the Prophets and depicts their message as something Jesus will personally fulfill. Jesus will bring all of Scripture to fulfillment in "his exodus that he was going to accomplish in Jerusalem" (9:31).

It is not as if every prophecy and every aspect of the law of Moses was simply a prediction about Jesus. The Law and the Prophets certainly spoke with divine inspiration to every generation that read them or heard them proclaimed, even long before the coming of Jesus. What they proclaimed, however, was a growing concern, a dynamic message concerning Israel's relationship with God. Jesus would fulfill Scripture by opening the door through his own "exodus" (his passion and resurrection) to the fullness of everything a relationship with God would ultimately mean.

Jesus calls his followers to prayer so that they might become privileged witnesses to his glory, a glory that also reveals what God has in store for those who hear the call and follow. Peter, James, and John witness his glory. Peter, at least, is euphoric from the mountaintop experience. He suggests building tents as something like shrines to the moment. But Peter did not understand what Moses and Elijah understood that the Messiah had to do in order to fulfill Scripture. Shortly after this revelation of his glory, Jesus reveals his commitment to his mission. The time has come to go to Jerusalem and he knows what awaits him there: his exodus.

The Way of the Cross

Luke 23:24-46

[23:24]The verdict of Pilate was that their demand should be granted. [25]So he released the man who had been imprisoned for rebellion and murder, for whom they asked, and he handed Jesus over to them to deal with as they wished.

[26]As they led him away they took hold of a certain Simon, a Cyrenian, who was coming in from the country; and after laying the cross on him, they made him carry it behind Jesus. [27]A large crowd of people followed Jesus, including many women who mourned and lamented him. [28]Jesus turned to them and said, "Daughters of Jerusalem, do not weep for me; weep instead for yourselves and for your children, [29]for indeed, the days are coming when people will say, 'Blessed are the barren, the wombs that never bore and the breasts that never nursed.' [30]At that time people will say to the mountains, 'Fall upon us!' and to the hills, 'Cover us!' [31]for if these things are done when the wood is green what will happen when it is dry?" [32]Now two others, both criminals, were led away with him to be executed.

[33]When they came to the place called the Skull, they crucified him and the criminals there, one on his right, the other on his left. [34][Then Jesus said, "Father, forgive them, they know not what they do."] They divided his garments by casting lots. [35]The people stood by and watched; the rulers, meanwhile, sneered at him and said, "He saved others, let him save himself if he is the chosen one, the Messiah of God." [36]Even the soldiers jeered at him. As they approached to offer him wine [37]they called out, "If you are King of the Jews, save yourself." [38]Above him there was an inscription that read, "This is the King of the Jews."

> ³⁹Now one of the criminals hanging there reviled Jesus, saying, "Are you not the Messiah? Save yourself and us." ⁴⁰The other, however, rebuking him, said in reply, "Have you no fear of God, for you are subject to the same condemnation? ⁴¹And indeed, we have been condemned justly, for the sentence we received corresponds to our crimes, but this man has done nothing criminal." ⁴²Then he said, "Jesus, remember me when you come into your kingdom." ⁴³He replied to him, "Amen, I say to you, today you will be with me in Paradise."
>
> ⁴⁴It was now about noon and darkness came over the whole land until three in the afternoon ⁴⁵because of an eclipse of the sun. Then the veil of the temple was torn down the middle. ⁴⁶Jesus cried out in a loud voice, "Father, into your hands I commend my spirit"; and when he had said this he breathed his last.

Pilate, as we find him in Luke, is a weak man, a pathetic judge. He knows he is condemning an innocent man, but the crowd has to be appeased. Pilate fears the crowd more than he loves justice. The crowd is not really of one mind, however. As much as Luke emphasizes how the people of Jerusalem have gone from hailing Jesus as their king (19:38) to demanding his death (23:21), Luke also pulls the curtain back from the tumult just far enough for us to encounter the women who are following Jesus on his way to his crucifixion, and they are mourning and weeping for him.

Luke says they are "lamenting" Jesus. This is Jesus' exodus, the one Moses and Elijah conversed about with him. Ironically, it is also his exile. The women know this; they may even be singing from the book of Lamentations. Simon has been pressed into taking up Jesus' cross behind him, and so Jesus plainly sees Calvary's height with every step he takes, but he pauses long enough to warn the women who are lamenting him that they should save their grief for themselves and for their children. In warning of the destruction that will come upon Jerusalem when it eventually revolts against Rome (AD 67–70), Jesus clearly knows and

recognizes the suffering that is in the world. He will not just suffer and die for them; he will suffer and die with them.

He also knows that death and destruction are not necessary. He came to Jerusalem knowing what would happen, not just to him, but apparently what awaited the city in its not-too-distant future. The warning signs of the coming destruction were in fact everywhere. The tension between Rome and the Jewish people had been smoldering for decades and did, quite frequently, erupt into violence. Every gospel tells us that Jesus clearly knew what awaited him upon his entry to Jerusalem. Luke graphically depicts Jesus yearning for a different fate for the city itself. Shortly after being hailed as a triumphant king he wept over the city.

> "If this day you only knew what makes for peace—but now it is hidden from your eyes. For the days are coming upon you when your enemies will raise a palisade against you; they will encircle you and hem you in on all sides. They will smash you to the ground and your children within you, and they will not leave one stone upon another within you because you did not recognize the time of your visitation." (Luke 19:42-44)

Jesus will suffer and die with criminals. The two he is crucified between are most likely insurrectionists. Some suggest they were like modern guerilla soldiers, zealots who thought the only good Roman was a dead Roman. In Luke, they give voice to the division Jesus promised he would create. "Do you think that I have come to establish peace on the earth?" Jesus asks in Luke 12:51. "No, I tell you, but rather division." At the very moment Jesus is dying, opening the door to salvation for all who will enter, one person mocks him and another beseeches him. The one who beseeches him is promised the gift of everlasting life.

Heaven and earth are moved at Jesus' death. The sun is eclipsed, the earth quakes. The veil in the temple that was meant to separate the holiest spot on earth from everything else is rent in two. This latter event poses a question whose answer is debated. Does the tearing of the veil symbolize the access to God that is now given to everyone through the death of Jesus, or does it suggest that the purpose of the temple itself has now been surpassed by something far greater? It's possible to interpret it both ways, and for all we know, Luke might even agree.

Jesus breathes his last, and in his last breath he commends his spirit to God. He has completed his journey.

These last moments of Jesus' life, his painful steps to an even more brutal and painful death, have drawn countless pilgrims of faith to reenact them. This happens, not just in ventures to Jerusalem as his footsteps are carefully followed along the Via Dolorosa, but in every Catholic church throughout the world as the Stations of the Cross are prayerfully remembered and ritually performed. If Jesus' death had been the final word on his life, however, it probably wouldn't be remembered at all. The memory of his suffering and death would have been swallowed up in all the other agonies of a world waiting for something to give it hope.

The **Stations of the Cross** is a devotional practice, still routinely held in churches during the season of Lent, that originated in the fourteenth century. Popularized by members of the Franciscan order, the Stations (or Way) of the Cross provides a way of meditating on the events associated with the passion of Christ and are likely modeled on various sites visited by pilgrims along the Via Dolorosa (the "Sorrowful Way") in the Holy Land. Although the number of Stations originally varied according to local custom, it was fixed at fourteen by Pope Clement XII in the eighteenth century. This beloved devotional practice allows followers of Jesus to "go on pilgrimage" within their own homes or parishes.

The Road to Emmaus

Luke 24:13-35

24:13Now that very day two of them were going to a village seven miles from Jerusalem called Emmaus, 14and they were conversing about all the things that had occurred. 15And it happened that while they were conversing and debating, Jesus himself drew near and walked with them, 16but their eyes were prevented from recognizing him. 17He asked them, "What are you discussing as you walk along?" They stopped, looking downcast. 18One of them, named Cleopas, said to him in reply, "Are you the only visitor to Jerusalem who does not know of the things that have taken place there in these days?" 19And he replied to them, "What sort of things?" They said to him, "The things that happened to Jesus the Nazarene, who was a prophet mighty in deed and word before God and all the people, 20how our chief priests and rulers both handed him over to a sentence of death and crucified him. 21But we were hoping that he would be the one to redeem Israel; and besides all this, it is now the third day since this took place. 22Some women from our group, however, have astounded us: they were at the tomb early in the morning 23and did not find his body; they came back and reported that they had indeed seen a vision of angels who announced that he was alive. 24Then some of those with us went to the tomb and found things just as the women had described, but him they did not see." 25And he said to them, "Oh, how foolish you are! How slow of heart to believe all that the prophets spoke! 26Was it not necessary that the Messiah should suffer these things and enter into his glory?" 27Then beginning with Moses and all the prophets, he interpreted to them what referred to him in all the scriptures. 28As they approached the village to which they were going, he gave the impression that he was going on farther. 29But they urged him, "Stay with us, for it is nearly evening and the day is almost over." So he went in to stay with them. 30And it happened that, while he was with them at table, he took bread, said the blessing, broke it, and gave it to them. ³¹With that their eyes were opened and they recognized him, but he vanished from their sight. ³²Then they said to each other, "Were not our hearts burning [within us] while he spoke to us on the way and opened the scriptures to us?" ³³So they set out at once and returned to Jerusalem where they found gathered together the eleven and those with them ³⁴who were saying, "The Lord has truly been raised and has appeared to Simon!" ³⁵Then the two recounted what had taken place on the way and how he was made known to them in the breaking of the bread.

The two disciples had hope once, but it is gone now, gone with the death of the one they had hoped would redeem Israel. They are leaving Jerusalem and the scene of the destruction, the death, of all their hopes. Little do they realize that they are pilgrims. How could they be? What is faith to them? They are leaving it all behind. But they are about to be surprised.

Jesus has died and been buried in a tomb, but that is not the end of the story. He has risen to a life that even Scripture is unable to adequately describe. In trying to describe what resurrection means, the First Letter of John has to admit that we have no clue, save one: "Beloved, we are God's children now; what we shall be has not yet been revealed. We do know that when it is revealed we shall be like him, for we shall see him as he is" (3:2).

These two downcast disciples meet Jesus on their journey, but they do not recognize him. He seems as a stranger to them, but this stranger listens to their conversation and asks them why they are troubled. The stranger seems surprised that the recent events in Jerusalem, which culminated in the death not only of Jesus but of all their hopes, have left them in sorrow.

In preparation for revealing himself to them, Jesus does two things of great significance for all of us. First, he opens Scripture to their understanding. The central message of Scripture is not obvious to just anyone; in fact, it takes Jesus himself to reveal it. These two disciples probably thought they had a good understanding of Scripture. After all, they had been hoping for the one who would redeem Israel, and that seemed like an important theme in Scripture. What they had missed in Scripture, however, was the message that redemption would come out of suffering, not as an escape from suffering. From beginning to end, through all the Law and Prophets, from the call of Abraham to the return from exile, Sacred Scripture whispers a patient message of waiting for the one who will finally transform the meaning not only of liberation and freedom, but of suffering, exile, and death as well. Those who help us find Christ and his passion and resurrection as the central message of Sacred Scripture for our lives are also sure signs that Christ himself continues to join us in our own journeys of faith. This message is what we listen for in every gathering of the faithful where Scripture is proclaimed. Finding the dying and rising of Christ in Scripture is far from Jesus' only message to these two disciples, however.

After Jesus breaks the word open for them, he also breaks bread with them, and it is in the breaking of the bread that the person behind the message of Scripture is ultimately recognized as being truly present with them. In the breaking of the bread they finally have eyes to see Jesus. What these two discovered in their journey is what we discover in faith at every Eucharist. Jesus is truly present to us in our assembly, in Sacred Scripture, and in the Eucharist.

Sojourners of the Dispersion

1 Peter 1:1-2, 17-19

¹:¹Peter, an apostle of Jesus Christ, to the chosen sojourners of the dispersion in Pontus, Galatia, Cappadocia, Asia, and Bithynia, ²in the

continue

foreknowledge of God the Father, through sanctification by the Spirit, for obedience and sprinkling with the blood of Jesus Christ: may grace and peace be yours in abundance. . . .

[17]Now if you invoke as Father him who judges impartially according to each one's works, conduct yourselves with reverence during the time of your sojourning, [18]realizing that you were ransomed from your futile conduct, handed on by your ancestors, not with perishable things like silver or gold [19]but with the precious blood of Christ as of a spotless unblemished lamb.

The First Letter of Peter is addressed "to the chosen sojourners of the dispersion." These words should be rich with meaning for us now. Sojourners, wanderers, pilgrims, exiles in the dispersion—these are the terms that mark us as people of God, terms that have marked the people of God for eons. From birth and baptism we are on a journey, for we have been called by God and to God we go. Peter has taken the Jewish understanding of the dispersion (the dislocation of the people of Judah into any of the world's other nations) and applied it to Gentiles who have embraced Christ in faith. By faith they belong to Christ who lives and reigns in heaven, and so their life on earth is one of sojourning in a place of exile. They await the fullness of life in the resurrection that is real in Christ but not yet a full reality for them.

And yet, as is the consistent experience of religious pilgrims, their lives have already been transformed. They have been ransomed from futility and given lives of purpose. Such a gift demands that they act with reverence throughout their lives toward the one who has given this new life to them.

Conclusion

Scripture immerses us in the experiences of those who have been called by God. Both their struggles to be faithful and the consequences of their failures have been carefully recorded. It is my hope that our examination of these selected passages has conveyed a message of encouragement for pilgrim people today. As Paul writes to the Romans (15:4), "For whatever was written previously was written for our instruction, that by endurance and by the encouragement of the scriptures we might have hope."

We are on a journey of faith, but we do not travel alone. In Hebrews we are reminded that we are surrounded by a cloud of witnesses who have undertaken the pilgrimage of faith before us (12:1). We began our study of many of these witnesses with the call of Abraham and Sarah. Looking back, we might recall that their journey of faith began not with them, but with Abraham's father, Terah. It is like this with us as well. For each one us, the journey through life, a life called to be an encounter with God, begins in the midst of the journey that others have undertaken before us. For many of us, our journeys are also the setting from which others, our children and grandchildren, will begin theirs. Along the way, our lives touch and are touched by the presence of many witnesses. No one undertakes a pilgrimage of faith alone.

What has not been mentioned so much in this commentary is the essential role that prayer must take in transforming life's venture into a true pilgrimage. Prayer springs from the realization that God is our companion during every step of the way. Even silence becomes a prayer with the realization that we never travel alone. Indeed, the God who promised Moses "I will be with you" (Exod 3:12), extends the same promise to us through Jesus: "I am with you always, until the end of the age" (Matt 28:20). The Lord be with you on your pilgrimage.

EXPLORING LESSON FOUR

1. What might have prompted Mary to visit her cousin Elizabeth immediately after the annunciation (Luke 1:39-40)?

_____

_____

_____

_____

2. According to the commentary, how might we best understand the meaning of the first verse of Mark's gospel: "The beginning of the gospel of Jesus Christ [the Son of God]"?

_____

_____

_____

_____

3. In what way did Mark's use of the word "gospel" challenge the political elite of his own time?

_____

_____

_____

_____

4. How is discipleship described in the Gospel of John? How do you understand what it means to "abide" or "stay" with Jesus (John 1:39; 15:4)?

_____

_____

_____

_____

5. a) How does Jesus' command to take up your cross and follow him characterize your earthly pilgrimage (Mark 8:34)? What does this way of life mean for you?

_____

_____

_____

_____

...early expects that our willingness to follow him must be our absolute top priority, ...s evidenced by his words to the disciple that wanted to bury his father (Matt 8:21). What challenge does this expectation pose to you?

_____

_____

_____

_____

6. What is the "exodus" that Jesus accomplishes in Jerusalem (Luke 9:31), and in what way is this exodus also an exile (see Luke 23:27-31)?

_____

_____

_____

_____

7. What possible explanations might be offered to explain the tearing of the veil in the temple upon Jesus' death (Luke 23:45)? Which interpretation of that event makes the most sense to you?

_____

_____

_____

_____

8. What was the message, embedded throughout Scripture, that the disciples on the road to Emmaus had missed (Luke 24:25-27)?

_____

_____

_____

_____

9. By addressing all Christians as "the chosen sojourners of the dispersion" (1 Pet 1:1), Peter recognizes that Gentile converts share in the salvation history of the chosen people. In what ways does the experience of Christians today recall the religious experiences of the Exodus and exile?

_____

_____

_____

_____

10. No one ever travels on the pilgrimage of faith alone; we are accompanied on our journey by companions, both earthly and supernatural. Who have been your companions on your faith journey thus far in life?

_____

_____

_____

_____

CLOSING PRAYER

Prayer

He summoned the crowd with his disciples and said to them, "Whoever wishes to come after me must deny himself, take up his cross, and follow me. For whoever wishes to save his life will lose it, but whoever loses his life for my sake and that of the gospel will save it." (Mark 8:34-35)

Lord Jesus, the road on which we travel is filled with obstacles. We struggle with sickness and grief; our minds are often burdened with anxiety and disappointment. Sin clouds our vision and hardens our hearts, and at times we are tempted to leave the path and forsake the journey altogether. In these times, we pray that you will strengthen us with your grace and direct our eyes to your cross. In imitation of you, may we take up our own crosses, bearing them without complaint. And may we remain with you and abide in you as we journey on this pilgrimage of faith. As our study comes to a close, we pray for one another . . .

SUGGESTED READING

Bergant, Dianne. *Israel's Story, Part One.* Collegeville, MN: Liturgical Press, 2006.

———. *Israel's Story, Part Two.* Collegeville, MN: Liturgical Press, 2007.

Binz, Stephen J. *The God of Freedom and Life: A Commentary on the Book of Exodus.* Collegeville, MN: Liturgical Press, 1993.

Brown, Raymond E . *The Birth of the Messiah: A Commentary on the Infancy Narratives in Matthew and Luke.* Anchor Bible Reference Library. New York: Doubleday, 1993.

Brueggemann, Walter. *Genesis.* James Luther Mays, editor. Patrick D. Miller Jr., Old Testament editor. Interpretation, A Bible Commentary for Teaching and Preaching. Atlanta: John Knox Press, 1982.

Byrne, Brendan. *A Costly Freedom: A Theological Reading of Mark's Gospel.* Collegeville, MN: Liturgical Press, 2008.

Davies, Gordon F. *Ezra and Nehemiah.* David W. Cotter, editor. Berit Olam Series. Collegeville, MN: Liturgical Press, 1999.

Forest, Jim. *The Road to Emmaus: Pilgrimage as a Way of Life.* Maryknoll, NY: Orbis Books, 2007.

Hanson, Paul D. *Isaiah 40–66.* James Luther Mays, editor. Patrick D. Miller Jr., Old Testament editor. Interpretation, A Bible Commentary for Teaching and Preaching. Atlanta: John Knox Press, 1995.

Hartin, Patrick J. *James, First Peter, Jude, Second Peter.* Daniel Durken, editor. New Collegeville Bible Commentary. Collegeville, MN: Liturgical Press, 2006.

Hawk, L. Daniel. *Joshua.* David W. Cotter, editor. Berit Olam Series. Collegeville, MN: Liturgical Press, 2000.

Johnson, Luke Timothy. *The Gospel of Luke.* Daniel J. Harrington, editor. Sacra Pagina Series. Collegeville, MN: Liturgical Press, 1991.

LaVerdiere, Eugene. *The Beginning of the Gospel: Introducing the Gospel according to Mark.* Vols. 1 and 2. Collegeville, MN: Liturgical Press, 1999.

McKenzie, John L. *Dictionary of the Bible.* New York: Macmillan Publishing Co., 1965.

Moloney, Francis J. *The Gospel of John.* Daniel J. Harrington, editor. Sacra Pagina Series. Collegeville, MN: Liturgical Press, 1998.

———. *The Living Voice of the Gospels.* Peabody, MA: Hendrickson Publishers, 2006.

Senior, Donald. *Matthew.* Abingdon New Testament Commentaries. Nashville, TN: Abingdon Press, 1998.

Wright, N. T. *Jesus and the Victory of God: Christian Origins and the Question of God.* Vol. 2. Minneapolis: Fortress Press, 1996.

PRAYING WITH YOUR GROUP

Because we know that the Bible allows us to hear God's voice, prayer provides the context for our study and sharing. By speaking and listening to God and each other, the discussion often grows to more deeply bond us to one another and to God.

At *the beginning and end of each lesson* simple prayers are provided for individual use, and also may be used within the group setting. Most of the closing prayers provided with each lesson relate directly to a theme from that lesson and encourage you to pray together for people and events in your local community.

Of course, there are many ways to center ourselves in God's presence as we gather together in groups around the word of God. We provide some additional suggestions here knowing you and your group will make prayer a priority as part of your gathering. These are simply alternative ways to pray if your group would like to try something different from those prayers provided in the previous pages.

Conversational Prayer

This form of prayer allows for the group members to pray in their own words in a way that is not intimidating. The group leader begins with Step One, inviting all to focus on the presence of Christ among them. After a few moments of quiet, the group leader invites anyone in the group to voice a prayer or two of thanksgiving; once that is complete, then anyone who has personal intentions may pray in their own words for their needs; finally, the group prays for the needs of others.

A suggested process:
In your own words, speak simple and short prayers to allow time for others to add their voices.

Focus on one "step" at a time, not worrying about praying for everything in your mental list at once.

Step One	Visualize Christ. Welcome him. Imagine him present with you in your group. Allow time for some silence.
Step Two	Gratitude opens our hearts. Use simple words such as, "Thank you, Lord, for . . ."
Step Three	Pray for your own needs knowing that others will pray with you. Be specific and honest. Use "I" and "me" language.

Step Four	Pray for others by name, with love.
	You may voice your agreement ("Yes, Lord").
	End with gratitude for sharing concerns.

Praying Like Ignatius

St. Ignatius Loyola, whose life and ministry are the foundation of the Jesuit community, invites us to enter into Scripture texts in order to experience the scenes, especially scenes of the gospels or other narrative parts of Scripture. Simply put, this is a method of creatively imagining the scene, viewing it from the inside, and asking God to meet you there. Most often, this is a personal form of prayer, but in a group setting, some of its elements can be helpful if you allow time for this process.

A suggested process:

- Select a scene from the chapters in the particular lesson.
- Read that scene out loud in the group, followed by some quiet time.
- Ask group members to place themselves in the scene (as a character, or as an onlooker) so that they can imagine the emotions, responses, and thinking that may have taken place. Notice the details and the tone, and imagine the interaction with the Lord that is taking place.
- Share with the group any insights that came to you in this quiet imagining.
- Allow each person in the group to thank God for some insight and to pray about some request that may have surfaced.

Sacred Reading (or Lectio Divina)

This method of prayer invites us to "listen with the ear of the heart" as St. Benedict's rule would say. We listen to the words and the phrasing, asking God to speak to our innermost being. Again, this method of prayer is most often used in an individual setting but may also be used in an adapted way within a group.

A suggested process:

- Select a scene from the chapters in the particular lesson.
- Read the scene out loud in the group, perhaps two times.
- Ask group members to ponder a word or phrase that stands out to them.
- The group members could then simply speak the word or phrase as a kind of litany of what was meaningful for your group.
- Allow time for more silence to ponder the words that were heard, asking God to reveal to you what message you are meant to hear, how God is speaking to you.
- Follow up with spoken intentions at the close of this group time.

REFLECTING ON SCRIPTURE

Reading Scripture is an opportunity not simply to learn new information but to listen to God who loves you. Pray that the same Holy Spirit who guided the formation of Scripture will inspire you to correctly understand what you read, and empower you to make what you read a part of your life.

The inspired word of God contains layers of meaning. As you make your way through passages of Scripture, whether studying a book of the Bible or focusing on a biblical theme, you may find it helpful to ask yourself these four questions:

What does the Scripture passage say?
Read the passage slowly and reflectively. Become familiar with it. If the passage you are reading is a narrative, carefully observe the characters and the plot. Use your imagination to picture the scene or enter into it.

What does the Scripture passage mean?
Read the footnotes in your Bible and the commentary provided to help you understand what the sacred writers intended and what God wants to communicate by means of their words.

What does the Scripture passage mean to me?
Meditate on the passage. God's word is living and powerful. What is God saying to you? How does the Scripture passage apply to your life today?

What am I going to do about it?
Try to discover how God may be challenging you in this passage. An encounter with God contains a challenge to know God's will and follow it more closely in daily life. Ask the Holy Spirit to inspire not only your mind but your life with this living word.

Lesson 3

t of geographic changes
- judahs were exiled to Babylon 500bc
- are we a society in exile?
    - are we letting society define life
    and ignore God

Sons of
Solomon   Israel   8 tribes in northern   - Israel
          Judah   resented
                        ─ 2 tribes of south   - Judah

present day Jews
think they are
from these

taken
by Syria
never
returned